The Selected Oracles of Nostradamus

The Selected Oracles of Nostradamus

By Michel de Nostradamus

Translated into American by Jacqueline M. Dilworth

SEJDB/Truckee River Books

Revised 10th anniversary edition of The Selected Oracles of Nostradamus

Cover Illustration: Nostradamus by David Tscheekar in charcoal conté and carbon

Digital Book Design by Jacqueline M. Dilworth

Cover Design by Dave Cherry

Font Linux Libertine

EBook Edition ISBN- 978-0-9856570-1-7

Translation Copyright © 2022 by Jacqueline M. Dilworth

This book is available in print at most online retailers.

For ____ they _____ and they _____

In memory of A.H, who got me started and saw more. I owe him words.

In memory of A.J.D, who I wish could see it.

Vera loquor, nec falsa loquor, sed munere cœli
qui loquitur DEUS est, non ego
NOSTRADAMVS.

Table of Contents

Introduction from 2012 edition — i

Nostradamus Again? Returning to Nostradamus and His Prophecies — v

A Short Biography of Nostradamus — xii

The Selected Oracles translated into American
Century I — 17

Century II — 25

Century III — 31

Century IIII — 41

Century V — 53

Century VI — 64

Century VII — 79

Century VII — 84

Century IX — 94

Century X — 105

The Selected Oracles in the original French
Centvrie I   121

Centvrie II   128

Centvrie III   134

Centvrie IIII   144

Centvrie V   158

Centvrie VI   170

Centvrie VII   186

Centvrie IX   201

Centvrie X   213

Version History   231

About the Author   235

Introduction

"The certainty of things past and present gives us confidence in things to come."

From the Mirabilis Liber, the first book of prophecies printed in French and Latin in 1523. Which was possibly put together by Nostradamus's father, Jaume de Nostradame, who may have inspired Nostradamus to write his Oracles.

The poems in the book you are about to read are highlights from Oracles of Nostradamus, the prophecies that can be attributed to him with some certainty. And these poems can be easily understood by people who aren't European history majors, historians, or scholars of classical literature I have read many books on Nostradamus, looked at websites dealing with him, and have tried to avoid the many movies, TV documentaries, and radio shows about him and his work and all this I've come to one conclusion. Everybody seems interested in what they have to say about Nostradamus, rather than what he actually wrote almost 600 years ago.

The reason why most books on Nostradamus are so large is the fact that they are filled with commentary, and the author's own prejudices, assumptions, and opinions on the simple four-line quatrains that make up his prophecies. This will contain only the poetry of Nostradamus, without commentary or my own opinion, allowing you, the reader to come to your own conclusion on the validity or non-validity of Nostradamus. I believe that the main text of what Nostradamus wrote as his oracles are contained in the ten centuries of quatrains, his letters, the sexains and the almanacs which were first printed from 1555 until his death in 1566.

As much as possible, I have translated the quatrains literally, while keeping in mind the fact that at heart, this is really interesting poetry. A quatrain is a four-line poem, written in English with ten syllables in one of the different poetic meters, or beats, where the last words of each line rhyme. In French, poetry is purely syllabic and either in lines of ten syllables or twelve syllables. Nostradamus wrote his quatrains in ten syllables The Oracles are divided into ten centuries, that is, ten sets of one hundred quatrains (Century 7 only has 42), these are my own translations, compared with several of the more literal translations. The main sources for my translation are the 1689 of Les vrayes centuries et propheties de Maistre Michel de Nostradamus published by Jean Volker in Cologne, Germany and the 1815 Propheties de Michel Nostradamus published by J.A. Joly of Avignon, France.

Nostradamus neither wrote and nor stated nothing about the world ending in 2012 Anyone who says that he did is making it up and is totally wrong. Even the ancient Mayans prophecies say the world is not ending in 2012, simply moving into a new cycle. If the world ended, then I wouldn't have to pay back my student loan or the mortgage on my house. According to Nostradamus, the world will end in the year 3797 AD (from to the letter that Nostradamus wrote to his son that is the introduction to The Oracles), so we have plenty of time to see if the Mayans are right and to see if Nostradamus is right too.

Nostradamus's Oracles are tremendously vague at best. At worst, they are surreal, quasi-mystical poetry that is almost nonsense. Many of his oracles are full of references to Greek and Latin mythology as well as European History. They are written in French and a combination of Latin and Greek, with mixed up words thrown in to confuse everything. At best, many quatrains that could be applied to several events in history and if you notice, many of those "experts" on Nostradamus can't agree on the prophecies that have happened and those that have not happened.

Eventually, I will translate all the quatrains of Nostradamus, along with his introduction to them, and include the French originals. I hope that through these translations, Nostradamus will be heard as honestly possible, with only one bias- that of allowing the reader to decide whether Nostradamus's prophecies are real or merely just fiction and cryptic, fascinating poetry.

The most interesting documentary on Nostradamus is The Man Who Saw Tomorrow by David L. Wolper and narrated by Orson Welles. I would also recommend the 1994 French bio-pic Nostradamus, which is a great movie and tells much of the truth about the man, his life, and the times in which he lived. As for books, read this one since it is Happy New Year now, and forever.

12/31/2011
8/8/2012
7/23/2013

Nostradamus Again? Returning to Nostradamus and His Prophecies

(and how they keep coming back, in my life at least)

An autobiographical introduction to the new edition of my Nostradamus translation

Nostradamus has always been a part of my life. In fact, he was there at the start of my life, along with Orson Welles's The Man Who Saw Tomorrow if a certain story is to be believed. For a fact I remember seeing that documentary when I was very young and it made me very, very curious. When they started to talk about the end of the world, after the movie, I went to get the family Bible (I was the only one who really used it. My grandpa gave it to us and I pored over the book, reading it and reading it. Looking at all the pictures and really appreciating them, especially the Carravagio paintings in the book.) to read Revelations. I was very young and very impressionable. But Nostradamus made a far greater impression than what I read in Revelations.

I have also had an affinity with French things all my life. Persian things too. Nostradamus is absolutely

French and he talks much about Persia and the Persians. Naturally, I learned French and I became very good at it. My curiosity led me to read Nostradamus's actual words. I was very surprised by what I read.

Most of the quatrains (a poetic stanza of four lines) are very obscure. It is very early Modern French and unless you have some grounding in Classical Roman and Greek mythology, European history and geography, reading it feels like grasping at straws. To practice my French, which I hold very dear, I began to read though all Ten Centuries of Nostradamus's prophecies and translate them into modern American English.

I began this work when I was a junior in College at The University of Nevada. As I sit here now that is 20 years ago, October of 2002. I was unemployed at the time and needed a something to occupy my time apart from reading, writing poetry, and trying to produce plays with one of the most dramatic people I ever knew. I went through each and every quatrain and decided if I would translate it or not. For every one or two I translated, there would be at least three or four I didn't. I did my work and finished the translation about a month later. I shared it with a few friends. Read some of the translations at poetry slams. Even had my laptop read them out loud at poetry slams. I never really got a sense of what people made of how people perceived what I doing, other than they thought it was weird. I may do this again soon.

After a while, I went on with my life. I didn't have time

for poetry, Nostradamus, or whimsy. It is after all, very much whimsical. I graduated from college. Tried to move to Oakland and The Bay Area. I had to come back to Reno for various reasons. I opened a bookstore to survive. I began my Master's Degree program and started to teach. Time passed. It was about 2011 when I began to think about Nostradamus again.

I had always wanted to finish my translation of Nostradamus. Go back and see what I could. His preface where he explains his methods, what he was writing about, and how far out he saw his prophecies go. Since I was young I wanted to write and publish books. Also, after going to various bookstores and looking at translations of Nostradamus I found that they either explained everything to the point that we weren't seeing Nostradamus's words or they were old-fashioned and unclear. I felt that the style and language of the translations hid the meanings of the words, more than anything else. As I explain in more detail in my original introduction, my goal in translation is clarity. I looked for my translation of Nostradamus to prepare it and publish it.

It took a few weeks to go ahead and do this. I learned how to create an e-book which can also be used to make a published book. I also got help from a friend to do this, as it was my first book. Many of the choices she made I disagreed with and changed, added the biography of Nostradamus I wrote for The Mystica online, which was an early online metaphysical encyclopedia that I wrote for and helped edit. I miss

Alan Hefner, who was a dear friend, and an accepting one. I need to finish editing his autobiography as it is a fascinating read. I wrote an introduction asked a friend to make an illustration for cover.

My dear friend David Tscheekar made a beautiful portrait of Nostradamus. The drawing was scanned for the book's cover and it was framed. David told me that one day, his drawing would be worth a lot. It already is worth so much to me. It is currently in my studio, where I do my radio show and write.

Soon after that I had a physical book and an ebook. I was so proud of it. There was an issue though, it was too small! Since I didn't translate all of Nostradamus and didn't include the original French quatrains, the book was no larger than 100 pages. This made selling it in certain bookstores in the Reno area difficult. I was even told to go sell the book in a "Made in Nevada" store since it wasn't a "book". I took that to heart and took my books back.

For years after I held onto copies of the original edition. Some of you may have one right now. I have one, which is heavily notated and edited. I sold them during my NADAdada art shows and gave them away so they could go their life. I also made an audio recording of my translation at Dogwater Studios, with my friend Rick Spagnola. My plan was to release the recording along with the book, so people could hear what I did. Life intervened in both positive and negative ways.

I moved to New Mexico and I packed up my life. I wasn't able to put out any more CDs or books while I went through the throes of life. I didn't really think about Nostradamus or anything creative at that point, apart from poetry that was cathartic to me at that time. I also became very clearly aware of myself and who I really am. This was the breaking point. And I realized that Nostradamus knew about such moments because he wrote about them – all his prophecies are about such times.

After I left New Mexico, I went to Goldfield, Nevada and spent three very important years there. I found myself stable again and in one place. I started to reevaluate where I was going and what I was doing in my life. That included my books, movies, and recordings. As I have transitioned and changed my name everything else has had to change in accordance. Much of that is beyond the scope of this essay, but I will likely discuss it elsewhere.

Since it's been ten years since the original publication of my translation of Nostradamus and I wanted to finally get it out with a new cover and many revisions. The cover is newly done by Dave Cherry. He used the original portrait done by David Tscheekar and made a new cover. It has my correct name and it looks excellent, it's more like what I wanted originally for my book, ten years ago.

As for the content of the book, I am adding this introduction and more. I've gone through each Century of prophecies and my translations. Since it's been almost 20 years since I first did this, I have become much better at translation and my understanding of medieval French is better. I've also added more quatrains because I've found more to translate and ponder. The new translation are more faithful to the original translations. That is the heart of these poems for me: wonder. I also include the original French quatrains in the back of the book. Should you wish to see the original quatrain and compare it to my own version.

I'm not sure I will come back to these poems. I have other translations I want to finish: Bad Flowers, Paris's Spleen, and The Little Prince. I also have ones I want to try like Pere Ubu and Maldoror. My first translation and my first book will be Nostradamus and it has a special place in my heart.

I hope that my translation of Nostradamus shows how much I care for the brilliant man. May you find something good in my reflection of his words. Love and Slack now and forever to you and yours.

Doktor Jacqueline M. Dilworth
October 31, 2022

A Short Biography of Nostradamus

Michel de Nostradame, better known by the Latinized version of his last name, Nostradamus (which means Our Lady, as in Mary the mother of Jesus), was born on December 14, 1503 in the village of St. Remy, Province, France. He came from a Jewish family who converted to Christianity and claimed descent from the Issachar tribe, one of the lost tribes of Israel which was famous for the gift of prophecy. His early education provided by his grandfather Jean, who taught him Greek, Latin, Hebrew, mathematics and astrology. During his adolescence, Nostradamus was sent to the city of Avignon where he studied philosophy until 1522 when he attended the famous University of Montpelier, in the city of Montpelier, studying medicine.

In 1525, Nostradamus was granted a license to practice medicine, and began to treat those who suffered from the bubonic plague. Nostradamus was famous throughout France and Europe for the ability to cure those who were considered incurable. His reputation became known to Julés-César Scaliger, a physician who invited Nostradamus to visit him in the town of Toulouse. The young Nostradamus was very impressed with Dr. Scaliger and decided to settle in the town of Agen, not far from Toulouse.

In 1534, Nostradamus married a woman of "High

Estate" and they had two children. However his happiness was short lived because around 1538 his wife and children died from the plague. Soon after, Dr. Scaliger challenged his credentials as a medical doctor and he was accused of heresy by the Papal Inquisition, because of a statement made years before. Nostradamus left Agen and wandered southern France for six years, caring for victims of the plague and studying the occult sciences. Finally in 1546, Nostradamus settled in the village of Salon de Craux, where he met Anna Ponce Genelle, he married her and they had six children.

As early as 1550, Nostradamus issued an almanac full of predictions, and did so for several years. In March 1555, he published the first seven centuries (100 sets of quatrains, not referring to 100 years) of his prophecies, containing predictions from his time to the end of the world, 3797 AD. Thus, Nostradamus again became famous throughout Europe for his predictions, so much so that the French royal family asked him to come to Paris to make astrological charts for the entire family. He found that all seven Princes would become kings and would die and that the King himself would soon die; as he also predicted in Century 1:35 for Henri II, the King and in Century 10:9 for Francis II who married Mary, Queen of Scots. After an audience with the King, Nostradamus quickly returned home, after being told the Justices of Paris were about to charge him with the crime of magic.

In his old age, Nostradamus suffered from gout and

severe arthritis, and by 1564 those diseases totally debilitated him. On June 17, 1566 Nostradamus made his will and predicted how he would die, "found white, and dead in the bed". On August 2, 1566 he died as just he had predicted. Nostradamus was buried in the local church in Salon, in an upright tomb with a beautiful marble plaque. He predicted that it would be opened (Century 9:7), and it was in 1798 by superstitious Revolutionaries, but was reburied soon afterward in a new tomb.

Works Cited:
Nostradamus from themystica.com http://www.themystica.org/mystica/articles/n/nostradamus.html
by Jacqueline M. Dilworth)
The Oracles of Nostradamus. Charles A. Ward. Charles Scribners and Sons, New York, 1891.
Encyclopedia Britannica, Eleventh Edition. Chicago. 1911.

Century I

This is the First Century by Nostradamus, first printed on May 4, 1555 in Lyons, France by Macé Bonhomme. This first edition contained the Preface to his son César and 353 quatrains. A reprint was done by Bareste in 1840, Nostradamus's original manuscript is lost.

1

Sitting alone at night in secret study;
it is placed on the brass tripod.
A slight flame comes out of the emptiness
making successful that which should not be believed in vain.

2

The wand in the hand is placed
in the middle of the tripod's legs.
With water he sprinkles both the hem of his garment and his foot.
A voice, fear; he trembles in his robes. Divine splendor; the spirit sits nearby.

3

When the litters are overturned by the whirlwind
and faces are covered by cloaks,
The republic will be troubled by new people,
From then, the reds and whites will judge wrongly.

4

By the universe he will be made a king,
Who will have peace and will not live long
Then the fisherman's boat will be lost
To be ruled to its greatest detriment.

5

They will be chased away by a long fight,
By the countryside they will be troubled the most:
Village and city will have a greater debate.
Carcassone, Narobonne will have theirs hearts tried.

6

The eye of Ravenna will be destitute
When at his feet the wings will fail
The two from Bress will make a constitution
Turin Derseil, the Gauls will trample

7

Arriving too late, the deed done
the wind against them: letters taken on the road
The 14 conspirators are a group
Rousseau will lead the enterprises.

8

How many times will the city of the sun be taken
Changing its laws barbaric and vain:
Your evil comes to you. No longer will you give tribute
Great Hadrie will revive your veins.

9

From the Orient will come the Punic heart
Harrying Hadrie and the heirs of Romulus
Accompanying the Libyan fleet
Maltan temples and close islands empty.

10

The serpent transported in an iron cage,
Where the seven children of the king are held:
The old ones and the fathers come from the bottom of Hell,
Crying to see the death of the fruit of their loins.

11

The movement of the senses, heart, feet and hands,
Will be agreed. Naples, Lyon, Sicily,
Swords, fire, water then the noble Romans
Drown, killed, dead by a debilitated head

12

It will soon be said of a false, fragile brute
From a low to high place quickly promoted
Then, instantly disloyal and weak–
The man who will rule Verona.

14

From the enslaved people, songs and demands,
princes and lords are held captive in prisons:
in the future, they will by headless idiots,
received as divine prayers.

16

A scythe with a pond, joined in Sagittarius
at its highest ascendant.
Plague, famine, death from military hands,
the century approaches its renewal.

17

For forty years the rainbow won't appear.
For forty years all the days it will be seen.
The arid earth will become more dry
and there will be great floods when it will be seen.

23

In the third month at dawn,
the Boar and Leopard meet on the battlefield[1].
The tired Leopard looks to heaven,
seeing an Eagle playing with the sun.

26

The great man will be struck by a thunderbolt in the day,
an evil deed foretold by a petitioner:
Following the prediction, another falls in the night
Conflict in Reims, London and Tuscan pestilence.

---

[1] (Nostradamus uses the words the field of Mars for a battlefield. JMD)

27

Under the oak tree of Gienne, struck by lightning,
not far from there is the treasure hidden.
That has been for centuries gathered there,
when found, a man will die, his eye pierced by a lock
spring.

32

The great empire will be totally transformed
for a small place, that will soon grow.
A place of infamy, exiled, accounted
where he will come to lay down his scepter.

35

The young lion will overcome the old one,
on the field of battle in a single fight:
In a golden cage, his eyes will be pierced
two wounds in one, then he dies a cruel death.

48

Twenty years of the moon's reign have passed
Seven thousand years, another takes her monarchy.
When the sun takes her days,
only then my prophecies
will be accomplished and complete.

50

Born from the three water signs,
a man who celebrates Thursday as his holiday[2]:
His renown, power, and rule will grow
by land and sea, bringing a tempest to the East.

60

An emperor born near Italy,
who will cost the empire dearly:
They will say when they see his people
that he is less of a prince, than a butcher.

61

The miserable unhappy republic
will be destroyed by a new magistrate:
their great hatred gained from exile
will make the Swiss break their important contract.

62

The great loss, alas! Will be done to learning,
before the sky of Latona perfected:
fire, large floods by more ignorant scepters
so many long centuries before it is remade.

63

The plague is past, the world is smaller
for a long time the lands will be inhabited peacefully:
People will travel safely over the sky, land, and sea,
then new wars will be incited.

---

[2] (as his holiday implies that is the day of this man's day of worship. JMD)

64
During the night they will think they have seen the sun,
when the half pig/half man is seen:
Noise, screams, wars fought in the sky.
The brute beasts will be heard to speak.

67
The great famine that I feel approaching
will often turn, in some places then become universal:
So grand and long that they will grab
the roots of trees and the child from the breast.

87
Earthshaking fire from the earth's center,
will cause tremors around the new city:
Two great rocks will war for a long time
then Arethusa will redden a new river.

91
The gods will make mankind see
that they will be the authors of a great conflict:
before the sky was seen full of swords and lances,
the ones on the left-hand side will be afflicted most.

Century II

This is the Second Century by Nostradamus. It was first published in 1555.

3

From the sun's heat on the sea,
the fish around Negrepont will be half cooked:
The local people will eat them,
when Rhodes and Genoa lack biscuits (food).

5

When fire and letters are enclosed in a fish,
from it will come a man who makes war.
His fleet will have come a long way
to appear near the Italian land.

6

Near the harbor and in two cities
will be two scourges,
the likes of which have never been seen:
Famine, plague within people thrown out by the sword
will cry for help from the great immortal God.

24

Wild beasts with hunger will cross the rivers,
the greater part of the battlefield will be against Hister.
In a cage of iron, the leader will be dragged
when the German child obeys no law.

28

The final one with the last name of the prophet
will take Monday as his day and rest[3]:
Traveling far in his frenzy
delivering a great people from subjection.

29

The man from the east will leave his seat,
passing through the Apennine to see France:
Crossing through the sky, the seas and snow
and he will strike everyone with his rod.

39

A year before the conflict in Italy,
Germans, French and Spaniards will be for the strong man:
the schoolhouse of the republic will fall,
where all, except for a few, will suffocate to death.

40

A little later, not a long interval
by land and sea a great tumult will be raised:
Much more great will be naval battles,
fires,
animals who will make more tumult.

---

[3] Monday is Diana's day/Moon's day. And he takes his day of worship on Monday JMD

41
The great star will burn for seven days,
the cloud will make the sun appear double:
the big mastiff will howl all night long
when the great pontiff changes his abode.

45
All the heavens cry for the one born androgynous
near the sky human blood shed
too late, by death, a grand people recreated
and late, the help arrives.

46
After great misery for man a greater one comes,
when the great cycle of centuries is renewed:
Raining blood, milk, famine, fire and plague,
in the sky will be seen fire, dragging a long tail of sparks.

57
Before the war the great man will fall,
the great one to death; a death too sudden and lamented.
Born imperfect, he will go the greater part of the way,
near the river of blood, the ground is stained.

60
The Punic religion changed in the east
the Ganges, The Jordan, The Rhone, The Loire and The Tagus changing when the mule's hunger is sated
the fleet is destroyed, blood and bodies swimming.

62

Mabus will die and then will come
a terrible destruction of man and beast:
Suddenly vengeance will be revealed,
one hundred, hands, thirst, hunger
when the comet runs past.

72

The Celtic Army in Italy vexed
for all sides conflict and great loss
The Romans fled, oh Gaul repelled!
by the Ticino, battle of the Rubicon unsure.

75

The call of the unwanted bird
heard on the chimney:
so high will the bushels of wheat
rise that man will eat man.

79

The beard burnt and black by ingenuity
will subjugate the cruel and proud people:
The Great Chyren will take from far away
all the captives taken by the banner of Selin.

81

By fire from the sky, the city nearly burnt
The Urn again menaces Deucalion
Sardinia boxed by the Punic flag
after Libra leaves her coach[4].

---

[4] Nostradamus uses the word Phaeton as coach. JMD

82

By hunger, the prey take the wolf prisoner
then, the assailant in extreme distress
the heir with the last one in front of him
The great man does not escape in the middle of the crowd.

89

A day will come when the two great leaders are friends
their great power will be seen to grow:
the New Land will be at its height of power
to the man of blood the number is reported.

91

At dawn, a great fire will be seen
noise and light seen going to the North:
'round the world death and cries are heard,
death along with weapons, fire, and famine waiting for them.

92

Golden fire seen in the sky from the Earth
From on high, the heir stuck down, marvelous deed done
great human murder: the nephew of the great man taken
Spectacles of death while the proud one escapes.

95

The populated lands become uninhabitable,
great disagreement in order to obtain lands:
Kingdoms given to men incapable of prudence,
then for the brothers, death and dissension.

96

A burning torch in the sky seen at night
near the end and the start of The Rhône
famine, steel: help too late
The Persians turn to take Macedonia.

98

One with blood on their face,
the next victim to be sacrificed,
Thunder in Leo, auguring the portent,
to be put to death by the fiancée.

Century III

This is the Third Century of quatrains by Nostradamus.
It was first published in 1555.

2

The divine word will give to the substance
that which contains heaven and earth,
occult gold in the mystic deed:
Body, soul, and spirit have all power
all is below his feet, as at the seat of heaven.

3

Mars and Mercury, and the silver all together
in the south, extreme drought
in deepest Asia, they will say the Earth shakes
then Corinth and Ephesus will be perplexed.

4

When they will be close, the fall of the lunar people
from one to another not so far away,
cold, dryness, danger on the borders
even where the oracle first started.

5

Near, far, the fall of the two great luminaries
who will fail between April and March
Oh, what a loss! But the great kind people
by land and sea will save everyone.

6

In the closed temple lightning will enter
the citizens hurt inside their fort
Horses, cattle, people, the wave will touch the wall
by famine and hunger, armed by the weakest ones.

10

From blood and hunger the greatest calamity
seven times coming to the ocean beach
Monaco from hunger, place captured, captivity
The Great One led by a crozier in an iron cage.

11

The arms fight in the sky for a long time
The tree in the middle of the city falls
The vervain cut, steel in the face of the fire
then the monarch of Hadrie falls.

16

An English prince marked in his heavenly heart
will pursue his rich fortune
of two duels, one will piece his gall
hated by him, well loved by his mother.

17

Mount Aventine will burn at night
The sky totally dark in Flanders
When the monarch chases his nephew,
the people of the church commit scandals.

21

At Conca by the Adriatic
appears a terrible fish
with a human face and aquatic fin
that will be taken without a hook.

23

If France passes out beyond the Ligurian Sea
You will see yourself enclosed in islands and oceans
Mohammed contrary, more than the Adriatic Sea:
You will chew the bones of horses and asses.

26

They will make copies of kings and princes
Augurers and false prophets elevated
Horn, a golden victim of dazzling azure
the omens will be interpreted.

27

Libyan prince powerful in the West
The French Arabs will be inflamed
educated in condescending letters,
he will translate Arabic into French.

31

On the fields of Media, Arabia and Armenia
Two grand armies will assemble three times:
Near the banks of the Araxes the host,
In the land of Suleiman the Great they will fall.

32

A large grave for the people of France,
will approach from Italy:
when war is near the German corner,
and in the land of Italy.

35

In the deepest part of Western Europe,
from poor people will be born a child:
who, by his speech will seduce many people,
his power grows greater in the Kingdom of the East.

44

When the animal tamed by man,
after great pains and troubles speaks:
the lightning so terrible for the rod,
will be taken from the earth and suspended.

45

The five strangers enter into the temple
Their blood will profane the land
To the Tolousans it will set a hard example
For the one who will come to exterminate their laws.

46

The sky of Plencus's city warns us
With clear signs and fixed stars
That the age of change is approaching
Not for its good or for its bad.

48
700 captives rudely tied up
Sorting out half to be murdered
The hope is coming shortly
But not until after the 15th death.

57
Seven times the British people will change
Tainted in blood for 290 years
Not free, supported by Germans
Aries doubts his Bastarnan pole.

58
Near the Rhine from the Norican mountains
will be born a great man of the people, too late.
He will defend Poland and Hungary,
and they will never know what became of him.

59
Barbarian empire by the third usurped
Put to death by the greater part of his blood:
By senile death the fourth by him hit
By fear that by blood he has not died.

61
A large number of troops and the crusader sect
Set themselves up in Mesopotamia
Near the river a light company
That such law will hold for enemies.

64
The Persian leader will take great "Olchade",
The trireme fleet against Mahometan people
From Parthia and Media, pillage the Cylades
Long rest at the large port of Ionia.

67
A new sect of Philosophers
Despising death, gold, honors and riches:
From German mountains they will not be limited
Following them will with power and crowds.

71
Those on the islands for a long time in a siege
Taking vigorous force against enemies
Those outside dead, overcome by famine
The greatest hunger, never seen before.

72
The kind old man buried alive
Nearby the large river by false pretense.
The new old man ennobled by riches
Taken on the road ransomed for all his gold.

76
Born in Germany many sects born
Approaching happily strong paganism,
The captive heart and small returns
They will return to pay the true tithe.

77

The third climate included under Aries,
the year 1727 in October:
the King of Persia taken by those of Egypt, battle,
death, loss: a great shame to the cross.

78

The Scottish chief with six from Germany
Taken captive by people from the Oriental sea
Traveling near the Rock of Gibraltar and Spain
Presently in Persia by the frightening new King.

84

The great city will be desolate
Not one of its inhabitants there
Wall, sex, temple and virgin violated
By iron, fire, plague, cannons, people will die.

85

The city taken by tricks and fraud
By means of a beautiful boy captured
Assault undertaken by Raubine by the Aude
He, and all others dead for being tricked well.

92

The world near its last period
Saturn again late for its return
Empire changed toward the Brodde nation
The eye taken out at Narbonne by Autour.

94

For five hundred years more someone will count him
The one who has the ornament of his times
Then he will give a great bolt of light
By him for this century made content.

95

The Moorish law, seen to fail,
followed by another more seductive:
The Dnieper will be the first to give way,
by gifts and words more appealing.

96

The Chief of Fossan will have his throat cut
By the leader of the bloodhound and the greyhound
The deed one by those from the Tarpeian mountain
Saturn in Leo. 13th of February.

97

A new law will occupy a new land,
around Syria, Judea and Palestine:
the great barbarian empire crumbles
before the century of the sun is finished.

98

Two royal bothers fight so bitterly
That between them the war will be mortal
Each of them will occupy strong places
Realm and life will be filled with their great quarrel.

100

The last one honored by the Gauls
The enemy's man will be victorious
Force and land in a moment explored
By an arrow shot the envious one dies.

Century IIII

This is the fourth century by Nostradamus. The first 53 quatrains were first published in 1555. The complete century appeared for the first time in 1557.

1
That of the rest of the blood not shed
Venice demands that help will be given
After waiting a long time
City opens at the first sound of the horn.

2
Due to death France takes a trip
Fleet by sea warning over the Pyrenees
Spain in trouble, military men marching
Some of greatest of Ladies lead away to France.

3
From Arras and Bourges the large banners of the Brodes
A greater number of Gascons will fight on foot
Those along the Rhone will bleed the Spanish:
Near the hill where Sagonte sits.

5
Cross, peace, one under the divine word
Spain and Gaul will be united together:
Great disaster near and very bitter battle
No heart will be so strong not to tremble.

6
By new clothes after the find is made
Malicious plots and machinations:
The first dead, he will prove it
Color Venice ambush

10
The young prince accused falsely
The camp falls into troubles and quarrels
The chief murdered for his sustenance
The scepter pacifies: then it cures scrofula.

11
The man who governs the great cape
Will be made to do some things
The twelve red ones will sully the celery
Under murder, murder will come to be done.

15
From where will they think hunger comes
It will come from there, where it is satisfied
The eye of the sea by another canine
From one to the other oil and wheat is given.

16
The free city of liberty made a slave
The asylum of dreamers and profligates
The King changes them to be not so dangerous
From one hundred they become more than one thousand

18

Some of the best learned in the facts of the heavens
Will be, by ignorant princes, condemned:
Punished by edict, chased like criminals
And put to death when found.

21

The changes will be very difficult
City, province from the change will gain
High heart prudently given, chased by a clever man
Sea, land, people, their state changed.

23

The legion in the marine fleet
Calcium, sulphur, magnesium, and tar burnt
The long rest in the safe place
Port Selin, Hercules, fire will consume them.

24

Under the sacred ground a faint voice
Human flame of the divine seen shining
It will taint the earth with holy blood
And the holy temples destroyed by impure ones.

25

Subtle bodies endlessly visible to the eye,
come to cloud the reason for their own purposes:
The body, with the forehead, senses and head invisible,
as the sacred prayers diminish.

26[5]

The great swarm of bees will come
So that no one will know where they came from
At night the ambush, the guard in the trees
The city saved by five madmen who are not nude.

27

Salon, Mansol, Tarascon, from the arch of six
Where the pyramid still stands
They will deliver the prince of Denmark
Redeemed honor in the temple of Artemis.

28

When Venus will be covered by the Sun,
under the splendor will be a hidden form:
Mercury will have exposed them,
by a rumor of war will be affronted.

29

The hidden sun eclipsed by Mercury,
will be placed second in the sky:
Hermes will be made of Vulcan's food,
the Sun will be seen purely, shining and golden.

---

[5] (This quatrain seems to be written in a combination of Italian, Romansch,

and French. This makes it more difficult to interpret than others. JMD)

30

More than eleven times the Moon doesn't want the Sun,
both raised and lowered in degree:
put so low that no one will sew gold,
after famine and plague the secret will be discovered.

31

The moon, in the middle of the night over a mountain,
the new wise man alone with his brain saw it:
With his disciples invited to be immortal,
eyes to the south, hands on his chest, his body in the fire.

32

The places and times of meat given to fish
The communal law will be made against it:
The elderly will hold it strongly then it will be taken from the middle
Lovers of all things put far away.

33

Jupiter joined more to Venus than the Moon,
appearing in a white fullness:
Venus hidden under the whiteness of Neptune
Mars struck by graven wand.

34

The grand man from a foreign land taken captive
Chained in gold, offered to King Chryen:
The man in Ausonia, Milan loses the war
All his army put to flame and sword.

35
The fire extinguished, the virgins will betray
The greater part of the new group:
Lightning in sword, with lance the lone kings will guard
Etruria and Corsica, at night throat cut

43
Weapons will be heard fighting in the sky:
in the same year divine are the enemies:
they wish to unjustly consult the holy laws,
by lightning and war many believers put to death.

45
By a conflict a king will abandon his realm
The greatest chief will fail when he is needed,
Death profligate, few will escape
All cut up, one will be a testimony to it.

49
Before the people blood will be shed
It will come far from the high heavens.
But for a long time, nothing will be heard,
The spirit of one alone will come to testify.

50
Libra will see Hesperian reign
From sky and earth a monarchy:
From Asia no one see armies that perished
Only seven will have the rungs of the hierarchy.

51

A cupidinous⁶ duke pursues his enemy
Enters into the phalanx, impeding it
In haste on foot, coming to follow them
That day will see a conflict by the Ganges.

54

From the name that no Gallic King ever had
Never until now so frightening a thunderbolt.
Makes tremble Italy, Spain, and the English,
Greatly attentive to women and foreigners.

55

When the crow on the tower joined with brick
For seven hours will not stop screaming:
Presaging death from a blood-stained statue,
Murdered tyrant, people pray to their gods.

58

A burning sun in swallowed in the throat
Etruscan land washed in blood:
The chief pail of water, leading his son away
The lady captive led to the Turkish land.

60

The seven children left in hostage
The third comes to kill his son
By his son, two will be pierced
Genoa, Florence will come to confuse them.

---

[6] Greedy.

62

A colonel with machinacious ambition
Will seize for himself the great army
Against his prince false intention
And will be discovered under his arbor.

63

The Celtic army against the mountain people
Who will be armed and whistling for the birds
Peasants will work fresh presses
All thrown on the sword's edge.

66

Under the false color of seven shaven heads
Will spread many explorers
Wells and fountains sprayed with poison
At the Genoese fort, humans devoured.

67

When Saturn and Mars burn equally
The strong, dry air, a long crossing
By secret fires, a great place in blazes from burning heat
Little rain, hot wind, wars, incursions.

68

In a place not far from Venus
The two greatest of Asia and Africa
From the Rhine and the Hister will have come
Cries and tears from Malta and the Ligurian coast.

72

The Attomiques by Agen and Estore
At Saint Felix will have their parliament
Those of Bazasa will come at a bad time
Promptly taking Condon and Marsan.

75

The one ready to fight will defect
The Chief adversary will obtain victory:
The rear guard will make defense
The failing ones dead in the white territory.

77

Selin monarch, Italy peaceful
Kingdoms united by the Christian king of the world
Dying he will want to lay in blessed land
After pirates have been chased from the waves.

80

By the great river a great ditch, earth dug up
In fifteen parts the water will be divided
The city taken, fire, blood, cries, conflict
And the greatest concern at the colosseum.

81

Promptly one will build a bridge of boats
The army of the great Belgian prince passes through on them
In the depths and not far from Brussels
Passed beyond and seven cut up by pike.

83

Nocturnal combat the valiant captain,
Conquered, few people will flee
His people emotional, sedition not in vain
His own son will besiege him.

84

A great man of Auxerre will die miserably
Chased by those once under him
Put in chains, under a rude cable
In the Summer of that year Mars, Venus, and the Sun are in conjunction.

85

The white coal will be chased by the black
Made prisoner taken to the cart
Moorish camel on twisted feet
Then the younger one will blind the falcon.

86

The year that Saturn will be conjoined in Aquarius
With the sun, the very powerful king
At Reims and Aix received and anointed
After conquests that will kill the innocent.

87

A king's son with many languages learned
Different from his senior of the kingdom:
His handsome father by the older son understood
Will kill the principal adherent.

89
Thirty of London secretly conspiring
Against their king, on the bridge the plan
He and his satellites taste death
A blond king elected, native of Frisia.

92
The valiant captain's head cut off
Thrown in front of his adversary
His body hanging from the yardarm of the ship
Confused fleeing by oars against the wind.

93
A serpent seen near the royal bed
Will be by the lady at night the dogs will not bark:
Then born in France a prince so royal
From heaven all the princes come to see him.

96
The older sister of the British Isle
15 years before the brother will be born,
because of her promise, procuring verification
She will succeed to the kingdom of balance.

97
The year that Mercury, Mars, Venus retrograde
The line of the great monarch will not fail:
Elected by Portuguese people near Gaudole.
That will reign in peace and grow very old.

99

The brave eldest son of a king's daughter
will drive the Celts far away:
He will use the thunderbolts, many in an array,
few and distant, then deep into the west.

100

From celestial fire on the royal edifice
When the light of Mars fails
Seven months a large war, dead people from maliciousness
Rouen, Eureux the King will not fail you.

Century V

This is the Fifth Century, which appeared in print in 1557.

1

Before the coming of Celtic ruin,
Inside the temple two will speak
Dagger to the heart then pike for one mounted on the steed
Without making noise they will bury the great man.

4

The large mastiff is chased from the city,
being angered by the foreign alliance,
after chasing the stag to the field
the wolf and bear will defy each other.

5

Under the shadowy pretense of removing servitude
People and city will be usurped by him
Because of the lies of the young prostitute they do worse
Taken to the field reading false poems.

7

The bones of the Triumvir will be found
Looking for a deep enigmatic treasure:
Those around there will not be resting.
Uncovering this thing of marble and metallic lead.

8

Living fire and hidden death will be let out
Within the horrible atrocious globes
At night the fleet turns the city to dust
The city on fire, the enemy amenable.

9

The great arch demolished to almost its base
By the chief captive his friend anticipated
Born by a lady with a hairy face
By astuteness the duke trapped by death.

11

Those of the sun will not cross the sea safely
Those of Venus will have all of Africa:
Their kingdom no longer occupied by Saturn
And the Asian part will change.

14

Saturn and Mars in Leo, Spain captive
By the Libyan chief trapped in a war
Near Malta, Herodde taken alive
And the Roman scepter by the rooster struck down.

16

For its such high price the Sabeans cry
Human flesh turned into cinders and death
At the island of Pharos Crusaders perturbed
When at Rhodes a specter will appear.

18

From grief the profligate unhappy man dies
His conqueress will celebrate the hecatomb:
Pristine law, free edicts rewritten
Wall and Prince on the seventh day fall.

23

The two contented ones will be united together,
When for the most part they will be conjoined with Mars:
The great man of Africa trembles in fear
Duumvirat disjointed by the fleet.

24

The realm and law under Venus raised up
Saturn will have dominion over Jupiter
The law and kingdom of the Sun left
By the Saturnians who endure the worst.

25

The Arab Prince, Mars, Sun, Venus, Leo
The reign of the Church succumbs to the sea
Toward Persia nearly a million
The true serpent invades Byzantium, Egypt

26
The enslaved people by Martial happiness
Will come on high to a great degree
Changing their prince, one born a provincial
Passing over the sea, an army raised in the mountains.

28
The arms hanging and the legs bound
Pale face, in the chest a hidden dagger,
Three who will be sworn in the melee
the steel will be unleashed against the great man of Genoa.

32
Where all is well, the Sun and Moon are good
It is abundant, its ruin approaching
From the sky it comes to change your fortune
To the same state as the seventh rock.

34
From the deepest part of the English West
Where the chief of the British Isles is
A fleet enters through Gyronne, by Blois
By wine and salt, fires hidden in barrels.

35
By the free city of the great sea of Selin
That brings again the stone in the stomach
The English fleet comes under the drizzle
A branch taken, the great man starts war.

36

The sister's brother in the quarrel and falsehood
Will mix dew in the mineral
On the cake given to the slow old woman
She dies tasting it, she will be simple and rural.

41

Born in shadows and a dark day
He will reign and be a good sovereign
His blood will be reborn in the ancient urn
Renewing the age of gold for brass.

44

On the sea the red will be taken by pirates
The peace by his manner troubled:
Ire and greed will be done in a false act
For the great pontiff the army will be doubled.

45

The grand empire will be totally desolated
And moved into the forest of the Ardennes
The two bastards by the oldest beheaded
Aenobarb, nose like a hawk, will reign.

46

By the red hats quarrels and new schisms
When the Sabine will be elected:
They will make great sophism against him
And Rome will be injured by the Albans.

48

After the great affliction of the scepter
Two enemies by them will be defeated
The African fleet will come to be before the Hungarians[7]
On land and sea horrible deeds done.

49

Not from Spain, but from ancient France
he will be elected for the trembling ship,
to the enemy he will make a promise,
who will, during his reign, cause terrible plague.

51

The people of Dacia, England, Poland,
and of Bohemia make a new alliance:
to pass out of the columns of Hercules
the Spanish and Italians make a cruel plot.

53

The law of the Sun and Venus contending
Appropriating the spirit of prophecy
Not one or the other will be heard
The grand Messiah's law will hold with the Sun.

54

From the Black Sea and Great Tartary
a king will come to see France,
passing through Alania and Armenia,
in his Byzantium he will leave his bloody rod.

---

[7] Hungary is landlocked. I'm not sure how this happens...JMD

55

From the country of Felix Arabia
There will be born one powerful in Mohammed's law
Vexing Spain, conquering Grenada
And more by the sea for the Ligurian people.

60

By the shaven head a very bad choice will be made
Then no more of his charge will pass through the gate
He will speak with such great fury and rage
That to fire and blood all the sex will be settled.

62

On the rocks one will see blood raining
Sun East, Saturn West
Near Orgon war, at Rome a great evil seen
Ships sunk and the Tridental taken.

65

Suddenly come, the terror will be great
The principals of the affair hidden:
And the lady on brass will no longer be seen
Then little by little the great ones will be angry.

66

Under the ancient edifices of the vestals
Not far from the ruined aqueduct.
The Sun and the Moon are the shining metals
Burning lamp, Trajan in gold engravings.

69
No longer will the great man be falsely sleeping
inquietude comes to take repose:
A phalanx of gold, azure, and vermillion drawn
Subjugating Africa, gnawing it to the bone.

76
In a free place pitching his tent
he will not live in any city
Aix, Carpentras, The Island, Volce, Mont, Cavillion
In all those places he will abolish his trace.

78
The two friends not allied for long,
in thirteen years they give in to the barbarian prince:
The two will lose so much,
that one will bless the bark of Peter and its leader.

80
Ogma will approach great Byzantium,
the barbarian league will be chased away:
Of the two laws the pagan one will fail
barbarian and freeman in eternal struggle.

81
The royal bird over the city of the sun
will give a warning in the night for seven months:
The eastern wall will fall, thunder lightning
in seven days the enemies at the gates.

82
At the conclusion of peace outside the fortress
No one will go out who is in despair:
When those of Arbois, Langres, against Bresse
Will have the mountains of Dole ambush of enemies.

83
Those who will have an enterprise to subvert
an invincible, unparalleled, powerful kingdom:
Will deceive, warn for three nights
when the great man reads his Bible at the table.

88
On the sand, by a hideous deluge
From other seas a marine monster is found:
Near the place will be made a refuge,
Holding Savona the slave of Turin.

90
In the Cyclades, in Perinthus and Larissa
in Sparta and all the Peloponnesus:
a great famine, plague from false dust,
it will last nine months all over the peninsula.

92
After the See has been held Seventeen years,
five will change in the same time:
then one will be elected at the same time
that the Romans will not be agreeable to.

93

Under the land of the round lunar globe,
When Mercury will dominate:
The isle of Scotland will make a luminary
That will confuse the English.

96

In the middle of the great world a rose
For new deeds public bloodshed:
To say the truth one will have a closed mouth,
Then help will come too late.

98

At the forty-eighth degree of climateric
At the end of Cancer such great dryness
Fish in the sea, rivers: lake boiled rapidly
Bearn, Bigorre in distress from fire in the sky.

Century VI

This is the sixth century by Nostradamus. It was first published in 1557.

2

In the year 580 or more or less,
One will wait for a strange century:
In the year 703 the sky in testimony
That several kingdoms one to five will make change.

3

River that tries the new Celtic heir
Will be in great discord with The Empire:
The young price with ecclesiastical people
Ousts the scepter of the crown of concord.

4

The Celtic river changes its course,
No longer will it flow in the city of Agrippina:
Everything changed except the old language,
Saturn, Leo, Mars, Cancer plundered.

5

A great famine caused by a pestilent wave
from rain the length of the Arctic pole,
Samarobrin one hundred leagues from the hemisphere,
they will live without law, free from politics.

7

Norway and Dacia, and the British Isles
by the united brothers will be vexed:
the Roman leader, issued from Gallic blood
and the forces repulsed into the forest.

8

Those who were in the realm for knowledge
At the royal change will be impoverished:
Some exiled without support, having no gold,
Letters and the lettered will not be at a high price.

9

In the sacred temples scandals will be done
They are counted as honors and commendations:
For one they will make engrave medals of silver and gold,
The end will be in a strange torment.

10

In little time the temples with colors
Of black and white and the two intermixed:
Reds and yellows will take theirs with them
Blood, land, plague, famine, fire extinguished by water.

11

The seven branches to three will be reduced,
the older ones will be surprised by death,
Fratricide will seduce two,
the conspirators, while asleep will die.

12
Raising armies to ascend to empire,
the Vatican will hold the royal blood:
Flemish, English, Spanish with Aspire
against Italy and France will fight.

18
By physicians, the great king is deserted
he lives by chance, not the Hebrew's skill,
He and his people put high in the kingdom.
Grace given to the people who deny Christ.

19
The true flame engulfs the lady,
who would want to set the innocents on fire:
Near the assault the army is enflamed,
When in Seville a monster in beef is seen.

20
The union feigned will be short of length
some of them changed most of them reformed:
in the vessels people will be suffering,
then Rome will have a new leopard.

21
When those of the Arctic pole united together,
in the East will be great fear and dread:
A newly elected man, supported by the great tremor
Rhodes and Byzantium will be stained with Barbarian blood.

22

In the land of the great heavenly temple,
a nephew in London by peace is murdered:
Then the ship will be schismatic
false freedom will be shouted abroad.

23

The spirit of the kingdom depreciates coins
And the people will rise again their king,
New holy peace, with terrible holy laws
Rapis[8] was never in terrible array.

24

Mars and the sceptre will be in conjunction
under Cancer will be a calamitous war:
a little later a new king will be anointed,
who, for a long time, will pacify the Earth.

27

Within the islands of five rivers to one.
By the crescent of the Great Chyren Selin:
Through the mists of air the fury of one,
six escaped, hidden in bundles of linen.

31

The king will find what he wanted so much,
when the prelate will be taken wrongfully.
The answer to the duke will make him angry,
who in Milan will put many to death.

---

[8]Rapis is likely an anagram for Paris. JMD

32
Treason, by rods beaten to death,
taken, overcome by his disorder.
Frivolous advice given to the great captive,
when Berich, by anger, will bite his nose.

33
His hand finally by Alus bloody,
unable to protect himself by sea:
between two rivers he fears the military hand,
the black angry one will make him repent.

34
The flying machine of fire
comes to trouble the great, besieged chief:
within there will be such treason,
that those abandoned will despair.

37
The ancient work will finish itself
From the roof evil falls on the great man:
An innocent one is accused of the crime and dies
The guilty one hides in bushes in the rain.

38

Enemies to the profligates of peace
After conquering Italy,
The black one, bloodied red, will be committed
Fire, blood shed, water by blood colored.

41

The second chief of the kingdom of "Annemark",
By those of Frisia and of the British Isles
Will spend more than 100,000 marks
Vainly exploiting the voyage in Italy.

42

Ogma will be left the kingdom
of great Selin, who will do even more:
through Italy his banner will be extended
ruled by cautious forgery.

43

A long time without having inhabitants,
Where the Seine and the Marne come to the water:
By the Thames and warriors tried
Those who guard it deceived in the repulse.

44

At night by Nantes a rainbow will appear
from marine arts they will arouse rain
In the Arabian Gulf, a great fleet will sink to the bottom
A monster in Saxony will be born of a bear and sow.

46

A just man will be sent back into exile
by pestilence to the borders of Nogseggle:
answering to the red one will mislead him
the king retreats to the frog and eagle.

47

Between two mountains the great ones assemble
letting go of their grudge secretly:
Brussels and Dole overcome by Langres,
at Malines to execute their plague.

49

From the warlike party led by the great pontiff,
will subjugate the borders of the Danube:
Chasing the cross by hook and crook[9], captives,
gold, jewels, more than 100,000 rubies.

50

Within the pit will be found the bones,
incest committed by the stepmother:
the state changed, one will demand fame and praise,
and Mars will attend as their star.

51

People assembled, to see a new spectacle
Princes and kings by many spectators:
Pillars and walls fall: but like a miracle
the king saved and thirty of those present.

---

[9]   Crookedly JMD

52

In place of the great one who will be condemned,
outside the prison, his friend in place:
The Trojan hope in six months, joined, born dead
The sun in the urn will be taken, rivers frozen.

53

The great Celtic prelate by the king suspected,
in the night he will fly and leave the kingdom:
By the fertile duke to his great British king
Byzantium to Cyprus and Tunis unsuspected.

54

At daybreak at the second crowing of the roosters
Those of Tunis, Fez, and of Bougie
By the Arabs, the king of Morocco captured
The year 1607, of the liturgy.

56

The feared army of the enemy Narbonne
Will strongly scare the Hesperians:
Perpignan empty by the blind man of Arbon,
Then, by sea, Barcelona will take up swords.

57

He who was well advanced in the kingdom
Having a red chief close the hierarchy,
Harsh and cruel and he will make much fear
Succeeding to the holy monarchy.

58

Between the two distant kings
When the sun by Selin clearly lost
Between the two indignant ones great simulty
So that the Islands and Sienna have their liberty restored.

60

The prince outside his Celtic land
Will be betrayed, deceived by the interpreter
Rouen, La Rochelle by those of Brittany
At Blayés port deceived by monk and priest.

61

The large folded carpet will not show all
But by half the most of the story:
Driven far from the kingdom he will seem harsh
So that all will believe his warlike act.

63

The lady alone in the kingdom living for a long time
Will lay on the bed of honor with the unique one
Experiencing seven years of sorrow
Then with long life with the kingdom in happiness.

66

At the start of the new sect
The bones of the grand Roman will be found,
A marble sepulcher will appear, covered
Earth quaking in April, badly buried.

70

Chief of the world, the great Chyren will be,
PLUS OVTRE[10]
behind loved, feared, dreaded: his fame and praise will surpass the skies
and with the one title, Victor, will be content.

72

By feigned fury of divine emotion,
the wife of the great one will be violated:
the judges wanting to condemn such a doctrine,
(she is a) victim to the ignorant people, sacrificed.

74

The one chased away will return to the realm,
her enemies found to be conspirators:
more than ever, her times will triumph,
three, and seventy to death assuredly.

77

By the false victory of the deceived
Two fleets one, Germany revolts
The chief and his son murdered in the tent
Florence, Imola pursued into Romania.

---

[10] plus ultra is a Latin phrase that means further beyond. JMD

78

Crying the victory of the great growing Selin
by the Romans the eagle will be demanded,
Pavia, Milan and Genoa will not consent
then, by themselves the great lord claimed.

80

From Fez, the regime will reach those of Europe,
their city on fire, and the blade will cut:
The great one of Asia by land and sea with a great troop
that blue, Persians, the cross driven to death.

81

Tears, cries and laments, howls, terror,
heart inhuman, cruel black and cold:
Lake of Geneva the isles, of Genoa the major ones
blood pouring out, hunger for wheat, mercy to none.

82

Through the deserts of the free and fierce
will come to wander the nephew of the great pontiff:
knocked out by seven with a heavy club,
by those who will occupy the chalice after.

84

The one who in Sparta, lame of foot, would not reign
he will do much by seduction
so that by the short and long he will be arraigned
since he gave his perspective against the king.

86

The great prelate one day after his dream,
interpreted opposite to its sense:
from Gascony a Monk will come unexpectedly,
who will cause the great Prelate of Sens to be elected.

87

The election made in Frankfurt
will be negated and nullified[11], Milan will oppose it
The closest follower will seem so strong
that beyond the Rhine into the marches they will break him.

88

A great kingdom will be desolate
Near the Ebro they will assemble:
Pyrenees mountains give him consolation
When in May lands will tremble.

89

Between two ships feet and hands bound
Face anointed with honey and with milk sustained
Wasps and flies, love from parents stopped
Cup-bearer false, chalice tried.

---

[11](In the second line the French the negation of the election is very, VERY clear. The results of the election are not going to be counted at all. Marches in the fourth line is not marshes, like in many translations. Marches are the border territories between the old Holy Roman Empire and other counties. JMD)

90

The disgrace stinkingly abominable
after the fact will be congratulated:
The great excuse for not being favorable,
that Neptune will not be incited to peace.

96

Great city to the soldiers abandoned
never was mortal tumult so close to it:
O, what hideous calamity approaches,
except for one offense, none spared.

97

Five and forty degrees the sky will burn
fire approaching the great new city:
Instantly great scattered flame jumps,
when one would demand of the Normans proof.

99

The erudite enemy will find himself confused
his great army sick and defeated by ambushes,
Pyrenees and Pennine Mountains will be denied to him
near the river they will find ancient rocks.

(100)
INCANTATION OF THE LAW AGAINST INEPT CRITICS

Those who read this verse, think of it maturely,
let the profane and the ignorant herd keep away:
far away all astrologers, idiots and barbarians,
may he who does otherwise will be subject to the
sacred rite.

Century VII

This is the Seventh Century by Nostradamus. It contains only 42 quatrains, the first 40 were first published in 1557, but the last two did not appear until 1568.

3

After France's naval victory
The Barcelonans, the Saillinons, and The Marseillais
thief of gold, the anvil closed inside the ball
those of Ptolon will consent to the fraud.

5

Wine on the table will be spilled
the third will not have what he claimed
Two times from the black one of Parma descended
Perouse will do to Pisa what he believed.

11

The royal child disapproves of his mother
eye, feet wounded, rude, disobedient,
the news for the Lady strange and bitter
more than five hundred of her people will be killed.

13

From the city, marine and tributary
the shaven head will take the satrapy:
chasing the sordid man who then will be against him
for 14 years he holds the tyranny.

22
The citizens of Mesopotamia
angry with their friends from Tarrasconne,
games, rites, banquets, all the people asleep
vicar at Rosne, the city taken and those of Ausonia.

24
The buried man will come from the tomb,
tied up with chains the strong man of the bridge:
poisoned with the eggs of a barbel,
the great man of Lorraine by the Marquis du Pont.

25
With a long war all of the army worn out
so that for soldiers they will not find money
instead of gold or silver, leather will be made into coins
Gallic brass, sign of the crescent moon.

28
The captain will lead a great heard,
on the mountain closest to the enemy,
surrounded, by fire he makes such a way
 all escape except for thirty put on stakes.

30
The bag approaches, fire, a great blood shed
Po, great rivers, cattlemen for the enterprise
from Genoa and Nice after a long wait
Fossano, Turin, taken at Savigliano.

32

From the Royal Mountain in small house one will be born
who digs and counts on becoming a tyrant
raising troops from the marches of Milan,
Favena and Florence drained of gold and men.

33

By fraud the kingdom deprived of forces
the fleet blockaded, passages for the spy
two false friends will come to rally
awakening hatred that for a long time slept.

34

In great grief the people of Gaul
hearts vain and light they will believe in temerities:
Bread, salt, no wine or water: venom or ale,
the greater captive, hunger, cold, want.

35

The great fish will come to complain and weep
having chosen, mistaken for an age
not wanting to stay with him
he will be deceived those who speak his language.

36

God, the heavens all the divine words in waves
carried by seven shaven redheads to Byzantium:
against the anointed three hundred from Trebizond,
two laws will be made and horror then belief.

40

Within barrels, anointed with oil and grease,
will be twenty and one, closed before the harbor,
by second death they will do great deeds:
winning the gates and killed by the guards.

41

The bones of the feet and hands encased
because of noise the house, for a long time uninhabited:
By digging in dreams they will be disinterred,
the house healthy and without noise inhabited.

42

Two people newly come take the poison
pouring it in the kitchen of the great prince:
by the scullion the two are caught in the act
taken by the man who thought to torture the old man to death.

Century VIII

This is the eighth century by Nostradamus, which was first published in 1568.

1

Pau, Nay, Loron will be more fire than blood
to swim in praise,
the great one flees to the confluence
The Magpies are refused entrance
Pampon, Durance will confine them.

5

An ornate shining temple will appear
the lamp and candle at Borne and Bretueil
for Lucerne the canton turns around
when one sees the great rooster (cock) in his coffin

10

A great stink comes out of Lausanne
they won't know the origin of the deed,
putting out all people from afar
fire seen in the sky, a foreign people defeated.

13

The crusader brother with wild love
will with Praytus kill Bellerophon,
the fleet for a thousand years, the frenzied woman
drinks the potion, after the two die.

14
The great credit of gold, silver abundance
will blind honor by lust,
the adulterer's offense will become known,
that will be to his great dishonor.

15
By Aqulion[12] great efforts by a manly woman
almost all Europe and the universe vexed
the two eclipses put into such a hunt
and by the Hungarians life and death reinforced.

16
At the place that Hieron built his ship,
such a large and sudden flood
that there will be on place or land to attack
the waters mount Olympic Fesulan.

17
Those at ease will be suddenly thrown down
by the three brothers the world put into trouble,
the marine City taken by enemies,
hunger, fire, blood, plague and all evils doubled.

---

[12](Aqulion – a poetic name Latin name for the northeast wind, so from the northeast. JMD)

20

The false message about the fake election
runs through the city stopping the pact
voices bought, with blood the chapel stained
one empire made smaller with another.

21

In the port of Agde three flags will enter
bringing the infection and pestilence, not faith
passing the bridge three million taken away,
and the bridge broken by resistance of a third.

23

Letters found in the queen's chests
not one signature without the name of any author[13]
by the police the offers will be hidden
no one will know who the lover will be.

25

Heart of the lover opened by furtive love
in the stream will ravish the lady,
the half injury will be counterfeited lasciviously
the father of each deprive body of the soul.

28

The copies of gold and silver inflated,
after the theft, were thrown into the fire
at the discovery all is exhausted and troubled.
In marble written, prescripts interjected.

---

[13] between the second and third lines in French, there is a rhyming pun with author and offer. JDM

29

At the fourth pillar that they made sacred to Saturn
by earthquake and flood split
under the building of Saturn an urn is found
gold taken by Capion then given back.

31

From the first great fruit of the Prince of Perquiere
will come a very cruel, wicked man.
Within Venice he will lose his proud glory
and will be led into evil by the youngest Selin.

32

Guard yourself, French king, from your nephew
who will do so much that your only son
will be murdered making his vows to Venus,
accompanied by night at three and six.

37

The fortress by the Thames
falls when the king is inside locked up,
near the bridge he will be seen in his nightshirt
the man facing death, then in the fort barred.

41

A fox elected without saying a word
playing the saint in public living on barley bread
afterward he is a tyrant after a coup
putting his foot on the throats of the greatest.

43

With the fall of the two bastards
the nephew of blood will take the throne
within Lectoure will be blows of darts
the nephew in fear will fold his flag.

44

The natural offspring of Ogma
from seven to nine turns off the road
to the king the longtime friend of the half man
Navarre must destroy the fort at Pau.

48

Saturn in Cancer, Jupiter with Mars
in Feburary Chaldondon salva terre
Fort Castallón on three sides besieged
near Verbiesque mortal conflict war.

54

Under the color of the marriage treaty
magnanimous act by the great Chyren Selin,
Quintin, Arras recovered in the journey
the Spanish make a second butcher's bench.

55

Between two rivers he will find himself ensnared
barrels and casks united to pass outward
eight bridges broken, chief stabbed many times
perfect children will be slit in the throat.

58

Kingdom divided by two quarreling brothers
take arms and the British name
The Anglican title will be told to beware
surprised by night, led by the Gallic air.

59

By two times risen, by two times put down
the East will also weaken the West
Its adversary after many battles,
routed by sea at the time of need failing.

60

First in Gaul, first in Romania
by land and sea by the English and Paris
marvelous acts done by that great band
violent terax loses Lorraine.

66

When the inscription D.M. is found
in the ancient cave by a lamp discovered,
law, king and Prince Uplian[14] tried
in the pavilion Queen and Duke under cover.

69

Next to the young angel the old one falls
and will rise up above him at the end
ten years equal to the most the old one falls again
of three two one, the eight seraphin.

---

14   (Ulpian was a famous ancient Roman lawyer and legal scholar. JDM)

70

He will enter villainously, meanly, infamously
tyrannizing Mesopotamia.
All friends made by the adulterous lover
the land is horrible, black in physiognomy.

71

The number of astronomers will grow to so many
chased out, banished, and books censored
The year 1607 by holy gatherings
that not one will be safe from the sacred ones.

73

A barbarian soldier strikes the great king
unjustly, not so far from death
the avaricious mother the cause of the act
conspirator and kingdom in great remorse.

74

In the new land, a king has come very far
while the subjects arrive to welcome him,
his treachery will do so much that to the citizens,
instead of a feast it is a reaping.

75

The father and son will be murdered together
The prefect in his pavilion
The mother at Tours belly swollen by a son
a verdure crèche with silk butterflies.

76
More Macelin than king in England
born in an obscure place by force he will have an empire:
coward without faith, without law bleeding the land
his time comes so close that I sigh.

77
The Antichrist very soon annihilates the three,
twenty and seven years of blood his war will last.
The heretics dead, captive, exiled,
blood, human bodies, ruddy water, hail on the earth.

78
A mercenary with a twisted tongue
comes to the sanctuary of the gods.
To the heretics, he will open the door
raising up the Church militant.

79
He who by iron loses his father born in a nunnery,
from the Gorgon by blood conceives anew:
in a foreign land will do anything to be silent,
he who burns himself and his child.

80
Blood of innocents of widow and virgin
so much evil done by the method of the Great Red one
holy images soaked in burning candles
terrified by fear, none will to be seen to budge.

81
The new empire in desolation
will change from the northern pole.
From Sicily will come the feeling
to trouble the tributary enterprise of Phillip.

87
Death conspired will come to its full effect
charge given and voyage of death
elected, created, received, defeated by them
blood of innocence in front of faith by remorse.

90
When one of the cross finds his senses troubled
in place of the sacred he will see a crowned bull
by the virgin the pig's place will be taken
by the king order will not be sustained.

95
The seducer will be put in a ditch
and tied up for some time,
the cleric unites the chief with his cross
the sharp right draws the content ones.

96
The sterile synagogue without any fruit
will be received by the infidels
the daughter of the persecuted man from Babylon
miserable and sad they will clip her wings.

97

At the end of Var the Pompotans change
near the river bank the three beautiful babies are born.
Ruin to the people when they are of competent age;
the kingdom's countryside is seen to change the most.

100

By the abundance of the shed tears
from high to low by low to the most high
with too much faith the game is lost
death by thirst with abundant deficiency.

Century IX

This is the 9th century by Nostradamus. It was first published in 1568.

1

In the house of the translator of Bourg
letters will be found on the table,
one eyed, red haired, white haired, hard headed take the course
who will change for the new constable.

6

An infinity of English in Guienne
occupying it in the name of Anglaquitaine,
from Languedoç Ispalme, Bordelais
which they will name after Barboxitaine.

7

He who opens the found monument
and does not come to close it promptly.
Evil will come to him and none will prove it,
better to be a king of the Bretons or Normans.

8

The lesser king will put his father to death
after the conflict of death very dishonest:
writing found, suspicion will bring remorse
when the chased wolf lays on the bed.

9
When the lamp burning with inextinguishable fire
is found in the temples of the Vestals
child finds fire, water goes through the sieve:
death of the water of Nîmes, Toulouse's markets fall.

14
Put in a flat place, the dyer's cauldron
wine, honey and oil built over furnaces:
they will be drowned, without saying or doing an evil thing
seven from Borneaux extinguished from the canon.

16
From Castle Franco the assembly comes out
the ambassador not agreeing makes a schism:
those of Riviera will be in the fight
and to the great gulf they will deny entry.

17
The third does worse than Nero,
how much valiant human blood will flow and be gone:
He will rebuild the furnace
the golden century dead, new king great scandal.

27
The ranger, the wind close to the bridge,
highly received, strikes the Dauphin
the old woodworker passes in the woods united
going out far beyond the borders of the duke's rights.

31

The trembling of the earth at Mortara
St. George half sunk to the bottom,
drowsy with peace, war arises,
in the temple at Easter, abysses opened.

32

Made of fine porphyry a deep column is found
under the base inscriptions of the Capitol:
Bones, twisted hair, the Roman force tested
The fleet agitated at the port of Methelin.

33

Hercules, King of Romans, and Annemark,
from Gaul three Guion lastnamed,
Italy trembles and the one of Saint Mark
First among all monarchs renowned.

36

A great king taken by the hands of a young man
not far from Easter confusion knife cut:
perpetual captives lighting found on the Husne
when the three brothers will wound and murder each other.

37

Bridge and mills in December fall
in such a high place The Garrone rises:
Walls, edifices, Toulouse turned over
that no one will know his place like a matron.

41

The great Chryen will seize Avignon,
from Rome, letters in honey full of bitterness.
The letter and embassy leave Chanignon,
Carpentras taken by the black duke with a red feather.

43

Near the landing point of the Crusader army
Ishmaelites will ambush them,
from all sides hit by the ship Rauiere
prompt attacks by the ten elite galleys.

44

Leave, leave Geneva all of you
Saturn from gold will change to iron
Faypoz will exterminate all against them
before their arrival the sky will show signs.

45

There will not be a soul to ask
Grand Mendosus will obtain his empire:
Far from the court will be countermanded
Piedmont, Picardy, Paris, Tuscany the worst.

46

Go, flee from Toulouse Red Ones
for the sacrifice to make expiation:
The chief of the evil under the shadows of pumpkins:
Death to strangle carnal omination[15].

---

[15] Another word for prophecy. JMD

48
The great city of the maritime Ocean
its environs (surroundings) of a swamp in crystal:
during the winter solstice and the spring,
will be tried by a frightening wind.

50
Mendosus will come to his high kingdom
putting behind him a little the Norlaris
The red pale one, the male in the interregnum
the youth afraid and Barbaric terror.

51
Against the red ones sects will band together,
 fire, water, iron the rope by peace will spoil,
at the point of dying, those who plot
except for one will ruin the entire world.

52
Peace comes at one side and war
never had it be perused so greatly:
men complain, women innocent blood on the land,
and this will be all through France.

53
The young Nero in three chimneys,
will put living pages to be thrown and burned
happy are those who will be far away from such acts
three of his blood will have him ambushed and dead.

57

In the place of DRUX a king will rest
and will look for a law changing an anathema:
during this time the sky thunders very strongly
bringing the new king to kill himself.

60

Barbarian conflict in the black Cornette
blood shed, Dalmatia trembles:
Great Ishmael will set up his promontory,
frogs tremble to help Lusitania.

62

To the great one of Cheramonagora
crusaders by rank will all be attached,
the pertinax oppi[16] and mandrake
Raugon let out on October the third.

63

Complaints and tears, cries and great howls
near Narbonne, at Bayonne and in Foix:
Oh, what horrible calamities and changes
before Mars revolves around a few times.

65

To the corner of Luna he will take himself
where he will be taken and put in a foreign land,
The unripe fruit will be a great scandal
great blame, to one great praise.

---

[16] persevering opium is the translation from Latin. JMD

66
Peace, unity, and change will be
estates, offices low high and high very low
preparing a trip, the first fruit (spawn) torment
war ceases, civil process, debates.

68
From Mount Aymar the noble will be obscured,
the bad will come from the junction of the Saône and the Rhône:
in the woods hidden soldiers on Lucy's day
there never has been such a horrible throne.

71
In the holy places animals seen with hair
with him that will not dare the day:
At Carcassonne propitious disgrace
he will be set for a more ample sojourn.

73
In Foix, enters the king with a blue turban,
reigning for less than a revolution of Saturn,
the king with a white turban, heart banished to Byzantium
Sun, Mars, Mercury near Aquarius.

74
In the city of Fertsod homicide,
done and done many oxen plowing without sacrifice,
return again to the honors of Artemis,
and to Vulcan dead bodies buried.

77
The kingdom taken the king conspires
the lady taken to death swearing by lot,
life for the queen and son denied,
and the mistress at the fort of the consort.

78
The Greek lady of beauty who is ugly,
made happy by countless suitors,
then transferred to the Hispanic kingdom,
taken captive dying a miserable death.

80
The duke will exterminate his own
sending the strongest to foreign places:
by tyranny Pisa and Lucca ruined,
then the Barbarians without wine will gather grapes.

81
The cunning king will understand his ambushes
from three sides enemies to assail him:
a strange number of tears from hoods[17]
the Lemprin of the translator will come to fail.

---

[17] The word that Nostradamus uses here is coqueluches, the hoods people would wear if they had whooping cough. JMD

83

Sun, twenty of Taurus, so great will the earth tremble
The great theatre filled, will be ruined:
the air, sky and earth darkened and troubled.
When the infidel calls on God and the saints.

84

The exposed king will perfect the sacrifice
after finding his origin
Torrent opening the tomb of marble and lead
of a great Roman with the Medusine symbol.

89

Seven years for Philip will be fortune prosperity
he will beat down the efforts of the Arabs,
then at his noon a perplexing backwards affair
young Ogma will obliterate his fort.

90

A captain of the great Germany
will come to give false help
king of kings, helper of Hungary,
so that his revolt will make a great shedding of blood.

92

The king will wish to enter the new city
they come to defeat it by their enemies
a captive falsely freed to say and perpetrate
the king to be outside, staying far away from the enemy.

94

Weak galleys will be joined together,
false enemies the strongest on the rampart:
the weak assailed Bratislava trembles,
Lubeck and Meissen take the barbarian side.

98

The afflicted by fault of a single one stained
against the party opposing:
to the Lyonnaise he will send word to constrain
they will be rendered to the great chief of Molite.

100

Naval battle will be overcome at night
the fire in ruined ships of the West:
new code the large colored ship
ire to the vanquished and victory in drizzle

Century X

This the 10th and last century by Nostradamus. It was first published in 1568.

1

To the enemy, the enemy faith promised
will not be kept, the captives kept:
one taken near death and the rest in their nightshirts
the rest damned for being supported.

3

After five the flock will not put one out
fugitive from Penelon let loose
false murmurs, help comes after,
the chief will then abandon the siege.

4

At midnight the leader of the army
will save himself vanishing suddenly,
seven years later his fame not blemished
to his return no one will say yes.

7

The great conflict that they are preparing for Nancy,
The Aemathien says "I subjugate all."
The British Isle by wine and salt anguished
Hem, mi. two Phi. will not hold Metz for a long time.

8
Index finger and thumb perfumes the forehead
from Senegalia the count to his own son,
The Myrnamee by many of first forehead
Three in seven days injured dead.

10
Stained with murder, enormous adulteries
Great enemy of the all the human race:
Who will be worse than his grandfathers, uncles, or fathers,
in steel, fire, water, bloody and inhuman.

12
Elected Pope, elected and mocked
sudden suddenly moved prompt and timid,
by too much goodness and sweetness provoked to perish
fear extinguished guiding the night of his death.

13
Under the food of ruminating animals
by them led to the stomach of the city of fodder,
soldiers hidden their arms making noise
tried not long from the city of Antibes.

14
Urnel Vaucile without council of his own
boldly timid, by fear taken captive,
accompanied by many pale whores
in Barcelona, converted by the Carthusian monastery.

15

Father duke old in years and full of thirst
on the last day his son denies the jug:
plunged into the well alive coming up dead
Senate to the thread the death long and light.

17

The foreign queen seeing her pale daughter
by a regret enclosed in the stomach:
Lamentable cries will come from Angoulême
and from the first cousins marriage foreclosed.

20

All the friends who will have belonged to the party,
for the rude in letters put to death and ransacked
goods for sale at a fixed price great neanty
Never were the Roman people so outraged.

21

Through the disdain of the king sustaining the lesser king
he will be murdered presenting the jewels to him[18]
the father of the son wants to make him seem like a noble
doing like the Magi did long ago in Persia.

---

[18] The king that is doing what to whom is unclear even in the original. JMD

22

For not consenting to divorce
that then afterwards will be seen as undignified:
The King of the isles will be chased by force
but in his place will be one who does not have the sign of a king.

24

The captive prince in Italy conquered
passing Genoa by the sea up to Marseilles:
By great effort of the foreigners he surrendered
safe from gunshot, barrel of the bee's liquor.

25

By the Ebro opening the passage of Bisanne,
far away from the Tagus will make a demonstration
the outrage will be committed in Pelligouxe
by the great lady seated by the orchestra.

26

The successor avenges his brother in law
occupying the kingdom under the shadow of vengeance,
slain obstacle his blood death vituperous
For a long time Brittany holds with France.

27

By the fifth and one great Hercules
they will come to the temple opening the hand of war
One Clement, Julius, and Ascanius going backward
The sword, key, eagle, never was such a grand pique.

30

Nephew and blood of the new saint come,
by the surname he will sustain arches and roofs
they will be chased out put to death chased in the nude
in red and black they will convert their green.

31

The holy Empire, comes into Germany
Ishmaelites will find open places,
Donkeys will also want Kerman
The supporters of earth all covered up.

32

The great empire everyone would want to live in
One obtains it and gives it to the others:
but a short time will be his reign and state
two years he will be able to sustain himself on the sea.

33

The cruel faction in long robes
will hide under their sharp daggers,
Seizing Florence the duke and the diphthong place
its discovery by the immature and flangnards.

35

One who is born after the king flagrant in ardent lust
to enjoy his first cousin:
Female clothing in the Temple of Artemis,
will be murdered by the unknown one of Maine.

36

After the King of stumps speaks of wars
The United Isle will hold him in contempt
Some years later gnawing one and pillaging
by tyranny the island changes price.

38

Happy love stages the siege not far
the barbarian saint will be at the garrisons:
Orsini Hadria for the Gaulois will make a pledge,
for fear given to the army of the Grisons.

40

The young born to the British kingdom,
that his dying father will recommend,
the one dead LONOLE gives him dispute
and from his son the kingdom demanded.

41

At the border of Caussa and Charlus
not very far from the bottom of the valley:
from Villefranche music to the sound of lutes,
surrounded by cymbals and great strings.

42

The humane reign of the Anglican[19] offspring
will make their kingdom united in peace,
war half captive in his cloister
a long time peace will by them be maintained.

---

[19] Nostradamus uses Angelic in the original.

43

Too many good times too much royal goodness
Done and undone prompt sudden negligence
lightly he will believe his loyal spouse false
he puts her to death by benevolence.

44

When a king will be against his own people
natives of Blois subjugate the Ligurians,
Memel, Córdoba, and the Dalmatians,
of the seven then the shadow gives to the king gifts and restless spirits[20].

46

His life will be the death of indignant gold villainy
he will not be the new Elector of Saxony
from Brunswick sending for a sign of love,
the false one gives to the people a seducer.

48

From the deepest part of Spain insignias
coming from the tip and ends of Europe,
Troubles pass near the bridge of Laigne,
its great army defeated by a small group.

49

Garden of the world near the new city,
in the road of the hollow mountains,
will be seized and plunged into the tank,
drinking by force water poisoned by sulfur.

---

[20] Lemures is the word Nostradamus uses, which was a restless spirit according to the Romans.

53

The three prostitutes for a long time will quarrel
the greatest will wait to listen to the least:
the great Selin will no more be her patron,
she will call him fire, shield white route.

54

Born into this world by a furtive concubine,
at two put high by the sad news,
by enemies she will be taken captive
and led to Malines and Brussels.

55

The miserable nuptials will be celebrated
in great joy but at the end unhappy
Husband and mother will disdain the daughter in law
The Apollo dead and the daughter in law more pitiful.

56

Royal priest his bow too low
a large flow of blood comes from his mouth,
the Anglican[21] kingdom a kingdom breathing,
a long time dead as a stump, alive in Tunis.

58

At the time of mourning the feline monarch
will make war on the young Macedonian:
Gaul shakes, the barque going to ruin
Marseilles tried in the West conversation.

---

[21] Again, Nostradamus uses Angelic here.

59

Inside Lyons 25 of one breathe
Five citizens Germans, Bressans, Latins:
Under a noble one will lead a long train,
and discovered by barks of mastiffs.

60

I cry for Nice, Monaco, Pisa, Genoa
Savona, Siene, Capua, Modena, Malta:
Above the blood and sword for a gift,
fire, the earth will tremble, water, unhappy
unwillingness.

62

Near Sorbia to assail Hungary,
The herald of Brudes will come to warn them:
Byzantine chief, Salon of Slavonia
to the law of Arabs he will convert them.

63

Cydonia, Ragusa, the city of Saint Jerome,
become green again with medical help:
son of the king dead by the death of the two heroes
The Arabs, Hungary will take the same course.

65

O vast Rome your ruin approaches
not by your walls, but by your blood and substance:
the one with acrid words makes such a horrible coach
pointed steel put in all up to the necks.

66

The chief of London by the kingdom of Americh[22]
The Isle of Scotland tested by frost:
King Reb will have so false an Antichrist,
that he will put all of them in the melée.

67

A shaking so strong in the month of May
Saturn, Capricorn, Jupiter Mercury in Taurus[23]
Venus also, Cancer, Mars in Virgo[24]
then hail larger than an egg will fall.

70

The eye by an object will swell greatly
so much and such burning that snow will fall:
Watered fields come to diminish
as the primate succumbs at Reggio.

71

The earth and air will freeze so much water
when they will come to celebrate on Thursday,
he that will be will never be as handsome
than the four who come to honor him.

---

[22] America? JMD

[23] The words that Nostradamus uses here are in beef, so Taurus. JMD

[24] Here, Nostradamus writes in the Nun, so in Virgo. JMD

72

The year 1999, seven months,
from the sky will come a great king of terror.
Bringing back to life the great king of the Mongols
after which Mars reigns happily.

73

The present time together with the past
will be judged by the great Jovialist,
the world lately will be tired of him,
and the disloyalty by the jurist clergy.

74

In the revolution of the great seventh number
accomplished at the time of the game of Hecatombe,
not far from the great age of the millennium
that the interred will come out of their tombs.

75

So much awaited he will never come back
within Europe, in Asia appearing
on of the league issued from great Hermes,
and above all Oriental kings he will grow.

78

Sudden joy to sudden sadness,
will be at Rome for the pregnant[25] graces
Grief, screams, sobbing, tears, blood, excellent jubilation
Contrary bands[26] busted and raided.

---

[25] The verb in French can mean pregnant or embarrassed...JMD

[26] This word could be contraband as well...JMD

79

The old roads will be embellished,
the one passes on them to Memphis rebuilt:
The great Mercury of Hercules fleur-de-lys,
lands made to tremble, sea and country.

81

Treasure put in a temple by Western[27] citizens
within which taken to a secret place,
the temple opens the hungry bonds.
Retaken, ravished, a horrible prey in the mist.

82

Screams, weeping, tears will come with knives,
seeming to flee, they will give them a final assault,
all around parks planted on profound plateaux
the living pushed back and murdered in moments.

83

The signal to battle will not be given,
from the park they will be constrained to leave
from Ghent the banner will be recognized
from him who will cause all of his people to be put to death.

85

The old tribune at the point of trembling
he will be pressed, captives not delivered:
the will, non-will, he speaks of evil timidly
by the law to deliver his friends.

---

[27] Nostradamus uses the word Hesperian here. JMD

86

Like a griffin comes the King of Europe
accompanied by those of Aquilon,
a grand army of the reds and the whites he will lead,
and they will go against the King of Babylon.

87

A great king will come to take the port near Nice
the great empire's death will be completed:
In Antibes he will put his heifer,
the sea will vanish all the plunder.

89

From brick to marble the walls will be redone,
seven and fifty peaceful years:
joy to the humans, the aqueduct renewed,
Health, times of great fruit and mellifluity.

90

One hundred times dies the inhuman tyrant.
Put in his place wise and carefree,
all the senate will be within his hand,
angered by an evil hothead.

91

Roman clergy the year 1609
at the start of the year you hold an election:
of the one grey and black issued from Campania,
Never was there one as malevolent as he.

92

Before the father the child will be killed,
the father afterward between ropes of bulrushes,
The people of Geneva will exert themselves,
the chief lying in the middle like a log.

93

The new bark will undertake voyages,
there and near they will transfer the Empire:
Beaucaire, Arles, will keep the hostages,
nearby two columns of Porphyry found.

94

From Nîmes and from Arles and Vienne condemnation,
not to obey the Hesperian edict:
it is for the laborers to condemn the great man,
six escape in seraphic habit[28].

95

To the Spains comes a very powerful king,
by sea and land subjugating the South:
this evil will cause the lowering of the crescent,
clipping the wings of those of Friday.

96

The religion of the name of the seas will win
against the sect of the son of Adaluncatif,
an obstinate sect, deplored, feared
the two wounded by Aleph and Aleph.

---

[28] Clothes, like a nun or monk would wear. JMD

97

Triremes[29] full of captives of all ages
times good for the bad, the sweet for the bitter:
Prey for the Barbarians far too hastily
cupidinous to see wailing in the wind the feather.

98

The clear splendor for the joyous virgin,
will shine no more, a long time without salt:
with merchants, ruffians, odious wolves
all pell-mell universal monster.

99

The end of the wolf, lion, ox and ass
timid dear will be with mastiffs:
sweet manna no longer falls on them,
more vigilance and watch for the mastiffs.

100

The great empire will be for England,
the most powerful for more than three hundred years:
large armies cross by land and sea,
the Portuguese will not be content.

---

[29] This is an ancient type of ship. JMD

The text in French

CENTVRIE I

Quatrain 1,1

Estant assis de nuict secret estude
Seul reposé sur la selle d'aerain;
Flambe exiguësortant de solitude
Fait prosperer qui n'est à croire vain.

Quatrain 1,2

La verge en main mise au milieu de BRANCHES
De l'onde il moulle & le limbe & le pied:
Un peur & voix fremissant par les manches:
Splendeur divine. Le divin pres s'assied.

Quatrain 1,3

Quand la licture du tourbillon versee,
Et seront faces de leurs manteaux convers:
La republique par gens nouveaux vexée,
Lors blancs & rouges jugeront à l'envers

Quatrain 1,4

Par l'univers sera faict un monarque,
Qu'en paix & vie ne sera longuement,
Lors se perdra la piscature barque,
Sera regie en plus grand detriment.

Quatrain 1,5

Chassés seront pour faire long combat,
Par le pays seront plus fort grevés:
Bourg & Cité auront plus grand debat,
Carcas Narbonne auront coeur esprouvéz.

Quatrain 1,6

L'oeil de Ravenne sera destitué,
Quand à ses pieds les ailles failliront:
Les deux de Bress auront constitué,
Turin Derseil que Gaulois fouleront.

Quatrain 1,7

Tard arrivé l'execution faicte,
Le vent contraire lettres aux chemin prinses:
Les conjurez xiiii d'une secte:
Par le Rousseau semez les entreprinses.

Quatrain 1,8

Combien de fois prinse cité solaire.
Seras changeant les loix barbares & vaines:
Ton mal s'approche. Plus sera tributaire,
La grand Hadrie recourira des veines.

Quatrain 1,9

De l'Orient viendra la coeur Punique
Facher Hadrie & les hoirs Romulides
Accompagné de la classe Libyque
Temples Mellites & proches isles vuides.

Quatrain 1,10

Serpens transmis dans la caige de fer,
Ou les enfans septaines du Roy sont pris:
Les vieux & peres sortiront bas de l'enfer,
Ains mourir voir de fruict mort & cris.

Quatrain 1,11

Le mouvement de sens, coeur, pieds & mains,
Seront d'accord Naples, Lyon, Sicille:
Glaves, feux, eaux puis aux nobles Romains
Plongez tuez mors par cerveau debile.

Quatrain 1,12

Dans peu dira faulce brute fragile,
De bas en haut eslue promptement:
Puis un instant desloyale & labile,
Qui de Veronne aura gouvernement.

Quatrain 1,14

De gent esclave chansons, chant & requestes,
Captifs par Princes & Seigneur aux prisons:
A l'avenir par idiots sans testes,
Seront reçus par divines oraisons.

Quatrain 1,16

Faulx à l'estang joint vers le Sagitaire,
En son hault AUGE de l'exaltation,
Peste, famine, mort de main militaire,
La siecle approche renouvation.

Quatrain 1,23

Au mois troisiesme se levant le soleil
Sanglier, Liepard au champ Mars pour combattre:
Liepard laissé, au ciel extend son oeil,
Un aigle autour de Soleil voit s'esbattre.

Quatrain 1,26

Le grand du fouldre tumbe d'heure diurne,
Mal & predict par porteur postulaire:
Suivant presage tumbe d'heure nocturne,
Conflict Reims, Londres, Etrusque pestifere.

Quatrain 1,27

Dessouz de chaine Guien du ciel frappé,
Non loing de là est caché le tresor:
Qui par longs siecles avoit esté grappé,
Trouve mourra, l'oeil crevé de ressort:

Quatrain 1,32

Le grand empire sera tost translaté,
En lieu petit, qui bien tost viendra croistre:
Lieu bien infine d'exigue conté,
Ou au milieu viendra poser son sceptre.

Quatrain 1,35

Le lion jeune le vieux surmontera,
En champ bellique par singulier duelle:
Dans caige d'or les yeux lui crevera,
Deux classes une, puis mourir, mort cruelle.

Quatrain 1,48

Vingt ans du regne de la lune passez,
Sept mil and autre tiendra sa monarchie:
Quand le soleil prendra ses jours lassez,
Lors accomplit & mine ma prophetie.

Quatrain 1,50

De l'aquatique triplicité naistra.
D'un qui fera le jeudi pour sa feste:
Son bruit, loz, regne, sa puissance croistra,
Par terre & mer aux Oriens tempeste.

Quatrain 1,60

Un Empereur naistra pres d'Italie
Qui a l'Empire sera vendu bien cher:
Diront avec quels gens il se ralie,
Qu'on trouvera moins prince que boucher.

Quatrain 1,61

La republique miserable infelice
Sera vastee de nouveau magistrat:
Leur grand amus de l'exile malefice,
Fera Sueve ravir leur grand contracts.

Quatrain 1,62

Le grande parte las que feront les lettres,
Avant le cycle de Latona parfaict:
Feu grand deluge plus par ignares sceptres,
Que de long siecle ne se verra refaict.

Quatrain 1,63

Les fleurs passés diminue le monde,
Long temps la paix terres inhabitées:
Seur marchera par ciel, serre, mer & onde:
Puis de nouveau les guerres suscitées.

Quatrain 1,64

De nuict soleil penseront avoir veu,
Quand le pourceau demi homme on verra:
Bruict, chant, bataille, au ciel battre aperceu:
Es bestes brutes à parler lon orra.

Quatrain 1,67

La grande famine que je sens approcher,
Souvent tourner, puis estre universelle:
Si grand & long qu'un viendra arracher,
Du bois racine & l'enfant de mamelle

Quatrain 1,87

Ennosigee feu du centre de terre.
Fera trembler au tour de cité neufue:
Deux grands rochiers long temps feront la guerre,
Puis Arethuse rougira nouveau fleuve

Quatrain 1,91

Les dieux feront aux humains apparence,
Ce qu'il seront auteurs de grand conflict:
Avant ciel veu serein espee & lance
Que vers main guache sera plus grand affiict.

CENTVRIE II

Quatrain 2,3

Pour la chaleur solitaire sus la mer,
De Negrepont les poissons demy cuits:
Les habitans viendront entamer,
Quand Rhod & Gennes leur faudra le biscuit.

Quatrain 2,5

Qu'en dans poisson, fer & lettre enfermee,
Hors sortira, qui puis fera la guerre,
Aura par mer sa classe bien ramee,
Apparoissant pres de Latine terre.

Quatrain 2,6

Aupres des portes & dedans deux citez
Seront deux fleaux, & onc n'apperceut vn tel,
Faim, dedans peste, de fer hors gens boutez,
Crier secours au grand Dieu immortel.

Quatrain 2,24

Bestes farouches de faim fleuues tranner;
Plus part du champ encontre Hister sera,
En cage de fer le grand fera treisner,
Quand rien enfant de Germain obseruera.

Quatrain 2,28

Le penultiesme du surnom du Prophete,
Prendra Diane pour son iour & repos:
Loing vaguera par frenetique teste,
En deliurant vn grand peuple d'impos.

Quatrain 2,29

L'Oriental sorrira de son siege,
Passer les monts Apennons voir la Gaule:
Transpercera le ciel, les eaux & neige,
Et vn chacun frappera de sa gaule.

Quatrain 2,39

Vn deuant le conflict Italique,
Germains, Gaulois, Espaignols pour le fort:
Cherra l'escolle maison de republique,
Où, hors mis peu, seront suffoqué morts.

Quatrain 2,40

Vn peu apres non point longue interualle,
Par mer & terre sera faict grand tumulte:
Beaucoup plus grande sera pugne nauale,
Feux, animaux, qui plus feront d'insulte.

Quatrain 2,41

La grandé estoille par sept iours bruslera,
Nuee fera deux soleils apparoir:
Le gros mastin toute nuit hurlera,
Quand grand pontife changera de terroir.

Quatrain 2,45

Trop du ciel pleure l'Androgin procree,
Pres du ciel sang humain respandu:
Par mort trop tard grand peuple recree,
Tard & tost vient le secours attendu.

Quatrain 2,46

Apres grand troche humain plus grand s'appreste
Le grand moteur les siecles renouuelle:
Pluye sang, laict, famine, fer & peste,
Au ciel veu feu, courant longue estincelle.

Quatrain 2,57

Auant conflict le grand tumbera,
Le grand à mort, mort, trop subite & plainte,
Nay miparfaict la plus part nagera,
Aupres du fleuue de sang la terre teinte.

Quatrain 2,60

La foy Punicque en Orient rompue.
Grand Iud, & Rosne Loyre & Tag changeront.
Quand du mulet la faim sera repue,
Classe espargie, sang & corps nageront.

Quatrain 2,62

Mabus plustost alors mourra, viendra,
De gens & bestes vn horrible defaite:
Puis tout à coup la vengeance on verra,
Cent, main, faim quand courra la comete.

Quatrain 2,72

Armee Celtique en Italie vexee,
De toutes pars conflict & grande perte:
Romains fuis, ô Gaule repoussée,
Pres du Thesin Rubicon pugne incerte.

Quatrain 2,79

La barbe crespe & noire par engin,
Subiuguera la gent cruelle & fiere:
Le grand Chiren ostera du longin.
Tous les captifs par Seline banniere.

Quatrain 2,81

Par feu du ciel la cité presque aduste,
L'vne menace encor Deucalion,
Vexee Sardaigne par la Punique fuste,
Apres que Libra lairra son Phae"ton.

Quatrain 2,82

Par faim la proye fera loup prisonner,
L'assaillant lors en extreme detresse.
Le nay ayant au deuant le dernier,
Le grand n'eschappe au milieu de la presse.

Quatrain 2,89

Vn iour seront demis les deux grands maistres,
Leur grand pouuoir se verra augmenté:
La terre neuue sera en ses hauts estres,
Au sanguinaire le nombre racompté.

Quatrain 2,91

Soleil leuant vn grand feu l'on verra,
Bruit & clarté vers Aquilon tendants:
Dedans le rond mort & cris l'on orra,
Par glaiue, feu faim, mort les attendants.

Quatrain 2,92

Feu couleur d'or du ciel en terre veu,
Frappé du haut nay, faict cas merueilleux.
Grand meurtre humain: prinse du grand le neueu,
Morts d'espactacles eschappé l'orgueilleux.

Quatrain 2,95

Les lieux peuplez seront inhabitables:
Pour champs auoir grande diuision:
Regnes liurez à prudens incapables,
Lors les grands freres mort & dissention.

Quatrain 2,96

Flambeau ardant au ciel soir sera veu,
Pres de la fin & principe du Rosne,
Famine, glaiue: tardue secours pourueu,
La Perse tourne enuahir Macedoine.

Quatrain 2,98

Celuy de sang reperse le visage,
De la victime proche sacrifiee,
Tonant en Leo, augure par presage,
Mis estre à mort lors pour la fiancee.

CENTVRIE III

Quatrain 3,2

Le diuin Verbe donra à la substance,
Cômpris ciel, terre, or occult au laict mystique:
Corps, ame esprit ayant toute puissance,
Tant soubs ses pieds comme au siege Celique.

Quatrain 3,3

Mars & Mercure, & l'argent ioint ensemble,
Vers le midy extreme siccité:
Au fond d'Asie on dira terre tremble,
Corinthe, Ephese lors en perplexité.

Quatrain 3,4

Quand seront proches le defaut des lunaires,
De l'vn à l'autre ne distant grandement,
Froid, siccité, danger vers les frontieres,
Mesme où l'oracle a prins commencement.

Quatrain 3,5

Pres loing defaut de deux grands luminaires.
Qui suruiendra entre l'Auril & Mars:
O quel cherré! mais deux grands debonnaires
Par terre & mer secourront toutes pars.

Quatrain 3,6

Dans temple clos le foudre y entrera,
Les citadins dedans leur fort greuez.
Cheuaux, boeufs, hômmes, l'onde mur touchera,
Par faim, soif, soubs les plus foibles armez.

Quatrain 3,7

Les fugitifs, feu du ciel sus les picques,
Conflict prochain des corbeaux, s'esbatans
De terre on crie, ayde, secours celiques,
Quand pres des murs seront les combatans.

Quatrain 3,10

De sang & faim plus grand calamité,
Sept fois s'appreste à la marine plage:
Monech de faim, lieu pris, captiuité,
Le grand, mené croc en ferree cage.

Quatrain 3,11

Les armes batre au ciel longue saison
L'arbre au milieu de la cité tombé:
Verbine rogne, glaiue, en face tison,
Lors le monarque d'Hadrie succombé.

Quatrain 3,16

Vn prince Anglois Mars à son coeur de ciel,
Voudra poursuyure la fortune prospere
Des deux duelles l'vn percera le fiel,
Hay de luy bien aymee de sa mere.

Quatrain 3,17

Mont Auentine brusler nuict sera veu,
Le ciel obscur tout à vn coup en Flandres
Quand le monarque chassera son neueu,
Leurs gens d'Eglise commettrôm les esclandres.

Quatrain 3,21

Au Crustamin par mer Hadriatique,
Apparoistra vn horrible poisson,
De face humaine, & la fin aquatique,
Qui se prendra dehors de l'ameçon.

Quatrain 3,23

Si France passe outre mert lygustique,
Tu te verras en isles & mers enclos.
Mahommet contraire, plus mer Hadriatique
Cheuaux & d'Asnes ty rongeras les os.

Quatrain 3,26

Des Roys & Princes dresseront simulacres,
Augures, creuz esleuez aruspices:
Corne, victume d'oree, & d'azur, d'acre,
Inrerpretez seront les extipices.

Quatrain 3,27

Prince libinique puissant en Occident.
François d'Arabe viendra tant enflammer.
Sçauant aux lettres fera condescendent
La langue Arabe en François translater.

Quatrain 3,31

Aux champs de Mede, d'Arabe, & d'Armenie
Deux grands copies trois fois s'assembleront:
Pres du riuage d'Araxes la mesgnie,
Du grand Soliman en terre tomberont.

Quatrain 3,32

Le grand sepulchre du peuple Aquitanique
S'approchera aupres de la Toscane.
Quand Mars sera pres du coing Germanique
Et au terroir de la gent Mantuane.

Quatrain 3,35

Du plus profond de l'Occident d'Europe,
De pauures gens vn ieune enfant naistra,
Qui par sa langue seduira grande troupe,
Sont bruit au regne d'Orient plus croistra.

Quatrain 3,44

Quand l'animal à l'homme domestique,
Apres grands peines & sauts viendra parler,
Le foudre à vierge sera si malefique,
De terre prinse & suspendue en l'air.

Quatrain 3,45

Les cinq estranges entrez dedans le temple.
Leur sang viendra la terre prophaner.
Aux Tholosains sera bien dur exemple,
D'vn qui viendra ses lois exterminer.

Quatrain 3,46

Le ciel (de Plencus la cité) nous presage,
Par clers insignes & par estoilles fixes,
Que de son change subit s'approche l'aage,
Ne pour son bien, ne pour ses malefices.

Quatrain 3,48

Sept cens captifs attachez rudement,
Pour la moitié meurtrir, donné le sort:
Le proche espoir vindra si promptement
Mais non si tost qu'vne quinziesme mort.

Quatrain 3,57

Sept fois changer verrez gent Britanique,
Taints en sang en deux cens nonante an
Franche non point par appuy Germanique
Aries doubte son pole Bastarnan.

Quatrain 3,58

Aupres du Rhin des montaignes Noriques
Naistra vn grand de gens trop trard venu,
Qui defendra Saurome & Pannoniques,
Qu'on ne sçaura qu'il sera deuenu.

Quatrain 3,59

Barbare empire par le tiers vsurpé,
La plus grand part de son sang mettra à mort:
Par mort senile par luy le quart frappé,
Pour peur que sang par le sang ne soit mort.

Quatrain 3,61

La grande bande & secte crucigere,
Se dressera en Mesopotamie:
Du proche fleuue compagnie legere,
Que telle loy tiendra pour ennemie.

Quatrain 3,64

Le chef de Perse remplira grande Olchade,
Classe Triteme contre gens Mahometiques:
De Parthe, & Mede, & piller les Cyclades.
Repos long temps au grand port Ionique.

Quatrain 3,67

Vne nouuelle secte de Philosophes,
Mesprisant mort, or, honneurs & richesses:
Des monts Germanins ne seront limitrophes,
A les ensuyure auront appuy & presses.

Quatrain 3,71

Ceux dans les isles de long temps assiegez,
Prendront vigueur force contre ennemis:
Ceux par dehors morts de faim profligez,
En plus grand faim que iamais seront mis.

Quatrain 3,72

Le bon vieillard tout vif enseuely,
Pres du grand fleuue par fausse soupçon:
Le nouueau vieux de richesse ennobly,
Prins à chemin tout l'or de la rançon.

Quatrain 3,76

En Germanie naistront diuerses sectes,
S'approchant fort de l'heureux paganisme,
Le coeur captif & petites receptes,
Feront retour à payer le vray disme.

Quatrain 3,77

Le tiers climat sous Aries comprins
L'an mil sept cens vingt & sept en Octobre,
Le Roy de Perse par d'Egypte prins
Conflit mort, perte: à la croix grand opprobre.

Quatrain 3,78

Le chef d'Escosse, auec six d'Allemagne
Par gens de mer Orient aux captif:
Trauerseront le Calpre & Espagne,
Present en Perse au nouueau Roy craintif.

Quatrain 3,84

La grande cité sera bien desolee,
Des habitans vn seul n'y demeurera
Mur, sexe, temple & vierge violee,
Par fer, feu, peste canon peuple mourra.

Quatrain 3,85

La cité prinse par tromperie & fraude,
Par le moyen d'vn beau ieune attrapé.
Assaut donné Raubine pres de LAVDE,
Luy & touts morts pour auoir bien trompé.

Quatrain 3,92

Le monde proche du dernier periode
Saturne encor tard sera de retour:
Tanslat empire deuers nation Brodde,
L'oeil arraché à Narbon par Autour.

Quatrain 3,94

De cinq cens ans plus compte lon tiendra,
Celuy qu'estoit l'ornement de son temps:
Puis à vn coup grande clarté donra,
Qui par ce siecle les rendra trescontens.

Quatrain 3,96

Chef de Fossan aura gorge couppee,
Par le ducteur du limier & leurier:
Le faict par ceux du mont Tarpee,
Saturne en Leo 13. de Feurier.

Quatrain 3,97

Nouuelle loy terre neuue occuper,
Vers la Syrie, Iudée & Palestine:
Le grand empire barbare corruer,
Auant que Phebés son siecle determine.

Quatrain 3,98

Deux royals freres si fort guerroyeront
Qu'entre eux sera la guerre si mortelle:
Qu'vn chacun places fortes occuperons,
De regne & vie sera leur grand querelle.

Quatrain 3,100

Entre Gaulois le dernier honnoré,
D'homme ennemy sera victorieux:
Force & terroir en nomment exploré,
D'vn coup de traict quand moura l'enuieux.

CENTVRIE IV

Quatrain 4,1

CELA du reste de sang non espandu,
Venise quiert secours estre donné.
Apres auoir bien loing te^ps attendu,
Cité liuree au premier cornet sonné.

Quatrain 4,2

Par mort la France prendra voyage à faire,
Classe par mer, marcher monts Pyrenees.
Espaigne en trouble, marcher gent militaire:
Des plus grands Dames en France emmenees.

Quatrain 4,3

D'Arras & Bourges, de Brodes grans enseignes,
Vn plus grand nombre de Gascons battre à pied,
Ceux long du Rosne saigneront les Espaignes:
Proche du mont où Sagonte s'assied.

Quatrain 4,5

Croix, paix, soubs vn accomply diuin verbe,
L'Espaigne & Gaule seront vnis ensemble:
Grand clade proche, & combat tres accerbe,
Coeur si hardy ne sera qui ne tremble.

Quatrain 4,6

D'habits nouueaux apres faicte la treuue,
Malice tramme & machination:
Premier mourra qui en fera la preuue,
Couleur venise insidiation.

Quatrain 4,10

Le ieune Prince accusé faussement,
Mettra en trouble le camp & en querelles:
Meurtry le chef pour le soustenement,
Sceptre appaiser: puis guerir escrou"elles.

Quatrain 4,11

Celuy qu'aura gouuert de la grand cappe,
Sera induict à quelques cas patrer:
Les douze rouges viendront sou"iller la nappa,
Soubz meurtre, meurtre se viendra perpetrer.

Quatrain 4,15

D'où pensera faire venir famine,
De là viendra se rassasiement:
L'oeil de la mer par auare canine
Pour de l'vn l'autre donra huyle, froment.

Quatrain 4,16

La cité franche de liberté fait serue.
Des profligez & resueurs faict asyle.
Le Roy changé à eux non si proterue:
De cent seront deuenus plus de mille.

Quatrain 4,18

Des plus lettrez dessus les faits celestes
Seront par princes ignorans reprouuez:
Punis d'Edit, chassez, comme scelestes,
Et mis à mort là où seront trouuez.

Quatrain 4,21

Le changement sera fort difficile,
Cité, prouince au change gain fera:
Coeur haut, prudent mis, chassé luy habile,
Mer, terre, peuple son estat changera.

Quatrain 4,23

La legion dans la marine classe,
Calcine, Magnes soulphre, & poix bruslera:
Le long repos de l'asseuree place,
Port Selyn, Hercle feu les consumera.

Quatrain 4,24

Ouy soubs terre saincte Dame voix fainte,
Humaine flamme pour diuine voir luire:
Fera des seuls de leur sang terre tainte,
Et les saincts temples pour les impurs destruire.\

Quatrain 4,25

Corps sublimes sans fin à l'oeil visibles,
Ob nubiler viendront par ces raisons:
Corps, front comprins, sens chefs & inuisibles,
Diminuant les sacrees oraisons.

Quatrain 4,26[30]

Lou grand eyssame se leuera d'abelhos,
Que non salutan don te siegen venguddos.
Denuech l'êbousq, lou gach dessous les treilhos
Ceiutad trahido per cinq lengos non nudos.

Quatrain 4,27

Salon, Mansol, Tarascon de SEX, l'are,
Où est debout encor la piramide:
Viendront liurer le Prince Dannemarç
Rachat honny au temple d'Artemide.

Quatrain 4,28

Lors que Venus du Sol sera couuert,
Soubs l'esplendeur sera forme occulte:
Mercure au feu les aura descouuert,
Par bruit bellique sera mis à l'insulte.

Quatrain 4,29

Le Sol caché eclipse par Mercure,
Ne sera mis que pour le ciel second:
De Vulcan Hermes sera faicte pasture,
Sol sera veu peur, rutiland & blond.

---

[30] (This quatrain seems to be a combination of Italian, Romansch, and French. Killer bees? Naked madmen? This is one of my favorite quatrains. JMD)

Quatrain 4,30

Plus unze fois Luna Sol ne vouldra,
Tous augmenté & baissez de degrez:
Et si bas mis que peu or on coudra,
Qu'apres faim peste, descouuert le secret.

Quatrain 4,31

La Lune au plain de nuict sur le haut mont,
Le nouueau sophe d'vn seul cerueau la veu:
Par ses disciples estre immortel semond,
Yeux au mydi, en seins mains corps au feu.

Quatrain 4,32

Es lieux & temps chair ou poisson donra lieu,
La loy commune sera faicte au contraire:
Vieux tiendra fort puis osté du milieu,
Le Panta chiona philon[31] mis fort arriere.

Quatrain 4,33

Iupiter ioinct plus Venus qu'à la Lune,
Apparoissant de plenitude blanche:
Venus cachee sous la blancheur Neptune
De Mars frappee & par la grauee blanche.

---

31 The first words in line four are transliterated Greek. JMD

Quatrain 4,34

Le grand mené captif d'estrange terre,
D'or enchainé au Roy Chyren offert:
Qui dans Ausone, Milan perdra la guerre,
Et tout son ost mis à feu & à fer.

Quatrain 4,35

Le feu esteint les vierges trahiront
La plus grand part de la bande nouuelle:
Foudre à fer, lance les sels Roy garderont
Etrusque & Corse, de nuict gorge allumelle.

Quatrain 4,43

Seront ouye au ciel armes battre,
Celuy au mesme les diuins ennemis:
Voudront loix sainctes iniustement debatre:
Par foudre & guerre bien croyans à mort mis.

Quatrain 4,45

Par conflict Roy, regne abandonnera,
Le plus grand chef faillira au besoing,
Mors profligez peu en reschapera,
Tous destranchés, vn en sera tesmoing.

Quatrain 4,49

Deuant le peuple sang sera respandu,
Que du haut ciel viendra esloigner.
Mais d'vn long temps ne sera entendu,
L'esprit d'vn seul le viendra tesmoigner.

Quatrain 4,50

Libra verra regner les Hesperies,
De ciel & tenir la monarchie:
D'Asie forces nul ne verra peries,
Que sept ne tiennent par rang la hierarchie.

Quatrain 4,51

Vn Duc cupide son ennemy ensuyure,
Dans entrera empeschant la phalange,
Hastez à pied si pres viendront poursuyure,
Que la iournee conflite pres de Gange.

Quatrain 4,54

Du nom qui onque ne fut au Roy Gaulois
Iamais ne fut vn foudre si craintif.
Tremblant l'Italie, l'Espagne & les Anglois,
De femme estrangiers grandement attentif.

Quatrain 4,55

Quand la corneille sur tout de brique ioincte,
Durant sept heures ne fera que crier:
Mort presagee de sang statue taincte,
Tyran meurtri, aux Dieux peuple prier.

Quatrain 4,58

Soloeil ardent dans le grosier coller,
De sang humain arrouser terre Etrusque:
Chef seille d'eau, mener son fils filer,
Captiue dame conduicte terre Turque.

Quatrain 4,60

Les sept enfans en hostaine laissez,
Le tiers viendra son enfant trucider:
Deux par son fils seront d'estoc percez.
Genues, Florence, les viendra enconder.

Quatrain 4,62

Vn coronel machine ambition,
Se saisira de la grande armee,
Contre son Prince fainte inuention,
Et descouuert sera soubs sa ramee.

Quatrain 4,63

L'armee Celtique contre les montaignars,
Qui seront sçeuz & prins à la pipee:
Paysans frez pouseront rost faugnars,
Precipitez tous au fils de l'espee.

Quatrain 4,66

Sous couleur fainte de sept testes rasces,
Seront semez diuers explorateurs:
Puys & fontaines de poisons arrousees,
Au fort de Gennes humains deuorateurs.

Quatrain 4,67

Lors que Saturne & Mars esgaux combust,
L'air fort seiché longue traiection:
Par feux secrets, d'ardeur grand lieu adust,
Peu pluye, vent chaut, guerres, incursions.

Quatrain 4,68

En lieu bien proche non esloigné de Venus.
Les deux plus grands de l'Asie & d'Aphrique,
Du Ryn & Hister qu'on dira sont venus,
Cris pleurs à Malte & costé Ligustique.

Quatrain 4,72

Les Attomiques par Agen & l'Estore,
A sainct Felix feront leur parlement:
Ceux de Basas viendront à la mal' heure,
Saisir Condon & Marsan promptement.

Quatrain 4,75

Prest à combattre fera defection,
Chef aduersaire obtiendra la victoire:
L'arriere garde fera defension.
Les defaillans mort au blanc territoire.

Quatrain 4,77

Selin monarque l'Italie pacifique,
Regnes vnis par Roy Chrestien du monde:
Mourant voudra coucher en terre blesique,
Apres pyrates auoir chassé de l'onde.

Quatrain 4,80

Pres du grand fleuue grand fosse terre egeste,
En quinze pars sera l'eau diuisee:
La cité prinse, feu, sang cris conflict mettre.
Et la pluspart concerne au collisee.

Quatrain 4,81

Pont on fera promptement de nacelles,
Passer l'armee du grand Prince Belgique:
Dans profondez & non loing de Brucelles,
Outre passez, detranchez sept à picque.

Quatrain 4,83

Combat nocturne le vaillant capitaine,
Vaincu fuyra peu de gens profligé:
Son peuple esmeu, sedition non vaine.
Son propre fils le tiendra assiegé.

Quatrain 4,84

Vn grand d'Auxerre mourra bien miserable.
Chassé de ceux qui sous luy ont esté:
Serré de chaines, apres d'vn rude cable,
En l'an que Mars, Venus & Sol mis en esté.

Quatrain 4,85

Le charbon blanc du noir sera chassé,
Prisonnier faict mené au tombereau,
More Chameau sur pieds entrelassez,
Lors le puisné sillera l'aubereau.

Quatrain 4,86

L'an que Saturne en eau sera conioinct,
Avecques Sol, le Roy fort puissant,
A Reims & Aix sera receu & oingt,
Apres conquestes meurtrira innocens.

Quatrain 4,87

Vn fils du Roy tant de langues apprins,
A son aisné au regne different:
Son pere beau au plus grand fils comprins,
Fera perir principal adherant.

Quatrain 4,89

Trente de Londres secret coniureront,
Contre leur Roy, sur le pont l'entreprise:
Leuy, satalites là mort de gousteront,
Vn Roy esleut blonde, natif de Frize.

Quatrain 4,92

Teste tranchee du vaillant capitaine,
Seza iettee deuant son aduersaire:
Son corps pendu de la classe à l'ancienne
Confus fuira par rames à vent contraire.

Quatrain 4,93

Vn serpent veu proche du lict royal,
Sera par dame nuict chiens n'abayeront:
Lors naistre en France vn Prince tant royal,
Du ciel venu tous les Princes verront.

Quatrain 4,96

La soeur aisnee de l'Isle Britannique
Quinze ans deuant le frere aura naissance,
Par son promis moyennant verrifique,
Succedera au regne de balance.

Quatrain 4,97

L'an que Mercure, Mars, Venus retrograde,
Du grand Monarque la ligne ne faillir:
Esleu du peuple l'vsitant pres de Gaudole.
Qu'en paix & regne viendra fort enuieillir.

Quatrain 4,99

Laisné vaillant de la fille du Roy,
Respoussera si profond les Celtiques,
Qu'il mettra foudres, combien en tel arroy
Peu & loing, puis profond és Hesperiques.

Quatrain 4,100

Du feu celeste au Royal edifice.
Quand la lumiere de Mars defaillira,
Sept mois grand guerre, mort gens de malefice
Rou"an, Eureux au Roy ne faillira.

CENTVRIE V

Quatrain 5,1

Avant venuëde ruine Celtique,
Dedans le temple deux palementerôms
Poignard coeur, d'vn monté au coursier & picque,
Sans faire bruit le grand enterreront.

Quatrain 5,4

Le gros mastin de cité dechassé,
Sera fasché de l'estrange alliance,
Apres aux champs auoir le cerf chassé
Le loups & l'Ours se donront defiance.

Quatrain 5,5

Soubs ombre feincte d'oster de seruitude,
Peuple & cité l'vsurpera luy-mesmes
Pire fera par fraux de ieune pute,
Liuré au champ lisant le faux poe"sme.

Quatrain 5,7

Du Triumuir seront trouuez les os,
Cherchant profond thresor aenigmaique.
Ceux d'alentour ne seroit en repos.
Ce concauuer marbre & plomb metalique.

Quatrain 5,8

Sera laissé feu vif, mort caché,
Dedans les globes horrible espouuantable.
De nuict à classe cité en poudre lasché,
La cité à feu, l'ennemy fauorable.

Quatrain 5,9

Iusques au fond la grand arq molué,
Par chef captif l'amy anticipé,
N'aistra de dame front, face cheuelue,
Lors par astuce Duc à mort atrapé.

Quatrain 5,11

Mer par solaires seure ne passera,
Ceux de Venus tiendront toute l'Affrique:
Leur regne plus Saturne n'occupera,
Et changera la part Asiatique.

Quatrain 5,14

Saturne & Mars en Leo Espaigne captiue,
Par chef Lybique au conflict attrapé,
Proche de Malthe, Herodde prinse viue,
Et Romain sceptre sera par Coq frappé.

Quatrain 5,16

A son haut pris plus la lerme sabee,
D'humaine chair par mort en cendre mettre,
A l'isle Pharos par Croissars pertubee,
Alors qu'a Rodes paroistra deux espectre.

Quatrain 5,18

De dueil mourra l'infelix profligé,
Celebrera son vitrix l'hecatombe:
Pristine loy, franc edit redigé,
Le mur & Prince au septiesme iour tombe.

Quatrain 5,23

Les deux contens seront vnis ensemble,
Quand la pluspart à Mars seront conionict:
Le grand d'Affrique en effrayeur tremble,
DVVMVIRAT par la classe desioinct.

Quatrain 5,24

Le regne & loy sous Venus esleué,
Saturne aura sus Iupiter empire
La loy & regne par le Soleil leué,
Par Saturnins endurera le pire.

Quatrain 5,25

Le prince Arabe Mars Sol, Venus, Lyon
Regne d'Eglise par mer succombera:
Deuers la Perse bien pres d'vn million,
Bisance, Egypte ver. serp. inuadera.

Quatrain 5,26

La gent esclaue par vn heur Martial,
Viendra en haut degré tant esslevee,
Changeront Prince, n'aistra vn prouincial,
Passer la mer copie aux monts leuee.

Quatrain 5,28

Le bras pendant à la iambe liee,
Visage pasle, au sein poignard caché,
Trois qui seront iurez de la meslee
Au grand de Genues sera le fer laschee.

Quatrain 5,32

Où tout bon est, tout bien Soleil & Lune
Est abondant, sa ruine s'approche.
Du ciel s'auance vaner ta fortune,
En mesme estat que la septiesme roche.

Quatrain 5,34

Du plus profond de l'Occident Anglois
Où est le chef de l'isle Britanique
Entrera classe dans Gyronne, par Blois
Par vin & tel, ceux cachez aux barriques.

Quatrain 5,35

Par cité franche de la grand mer Seline
Qui porte encores à l'estomach la pierre,
Angloise classe viendra sous la bruine
Vn rameau prendre, du grand ouuerte guerre.

Quatrain 5,36

De soeur le frere par simulte faintise
Viendra mesler rosee en myneral:
Sur la placente donne à veille tardiue,
Meurt le goustant sera simple & rural.

Quatrain 5,41

Nay sous les ombres & iournee nocturne,
Sera en regne & bonté souueraine:
Fera renaistre son sang de l'antique vrne,
Renouuellant siecle d'or pour l'airain.

Quatrain 5,44

Par mer le rouge sera prins de pyrates,
La paix sera par son moyen troublee:
L'ire & l'auare commettra par fainct acte,
Au grand Pontife sera l'armee doublee.

Quatrain 5,45

Le grand Empire sera tost desolé
Et translaté pres d'arduenne silue:
Les deux bastards par l'aisné decollé,
Et regnera Aenodarb, nez de milue.

Quatrain 5,46

Par chapeaux rouges querelles & nouueaux scismes
Quand on aura esleu le Sabinois:
On produira contre luy grands sophismes,
Et sera Rome lesee par Albanois.

Quatrain 5,48

Apres la grande affliction du sceptre,
Deux ennemis par eux seront defaicts:
Classe Affrique aux Pannons viendra naistre,
Par mer terre seront horribles faicts.

Quatrain 5,49

Nul de l'Espagne, mais de l'antique France
Ne sera esleu pour le tremblant nacelle
A l'ennemy sera faicte fiance,
Qui dans son regne sera peste cruelle.

Quatrain 5,53

La loy du Sol & Venus contendus
Appropriant l'esprit de prophetie:
Ne l'vn ne l'autre ne seront entendus,
Par sol tiendra la loy du grand Messie.

Quatrain 5,55

De la Felice Arabie contrade,
N'aistra puissant de loy Mahometique:
Vexer l'Espagne, conquester la Grenade,
Et plus par mer à la gent Lygustique.

Quatrain 5,60

Par teste rase viendra bien mal eslire,
Plus que sa charge ne porter passera.
Si grande fureur & rage fera dire,
Qu'à feu & sang tout sexe trenchera.

Quatrain 5,62

Sur les rochers sang on verra pleuuoir,
Sol Orient Saturne Occidental:
Pres d'Orgon guerre à Rome grand mal voir,
Nefs parfondrees, & prins Tridental.

Quatrain 5,65

Subit venu l'effrayeur sera grande,
Des principaux de l'affaire cachez:
Et dame en brasse plus ne sera en veu"e,
Ce peu à peu seront les grands fachez.

Quatrain 5,66

Sous les antiques edifices vestaux,
Non esloignez d'aqueduct ruyne.
De Sol & lune sont les luisans metaux,
Ardente lampe, Traian d'or burine.

Quatrain 5,69

Plus ne sera le grand en feux sommeil,
L'inquietude viendra prendre repos:
Dresser phalange d'or, azur & vermeil
Subiuger Afrique la ronger iusques os.

Quatrain 5,76

En lieu libre tendra son pauillon,
Et ne voudra en citez prendre place
Aix, Carpen l'isle volce, mont, Cauaillon,
Par tous ses lieux abolira la trasse.

Quatrain 5,78

Les deux vnis ne tiendront longuement,
Et dans treize ans au Barbare Strappe,
Aux deux costez feront tel perdement,
Qu'vn benira le Barque & sa cappe.

Quatrain 5,80

Logmion grande Bisance approchera.
Chassee sera la barbarique Ligue:
Des deux loix l'vne l'estinique laschera,
Barbare & franche en perpetuelle brigue.

Quatrain 5,81

L'oiseau royal sur la cité solaire,
Sept moys deuant fera nocturne augure:
Mur d'Orient cherra tonnerre esclaire,
Sept iours aux portes les ennemis à l'heure.

Quatrain 5,82

Au conclud pache hors la forteresse,
Ne sortira celuy en desespoir mis:
Quant ceux d'Arbois, de Langres, contre Bresse,
Auront mons Dolle bouscade d'ennemis.

Quatrain 5,83

Ceux qui auront entreprins subuertir,
Nompareil regne, puissant & inuincible:
Feront par fraudes, nuicts trois aduertir,
Quand le plus grand à table lira Bible.

Quatrain 5,88

Sur le sablon par vn hideux deluge,
Des autres mers trouué monstre marin:
Proche du lieu sera faicte vn refuge,
Venant Sauone esclaue de Turin.

Quatrain 5,90

Dans le cyclades, en printhe & larisse,
Dedans Sparte tout le Peloponnesse:
Si grand famine, peste par faux connisse,
Neuf mois tiendra & tout le cheronnesse.

Quatrain 5,92

Apres le siege tenu dixscept ans,
Cinq changeront en tel reuolu terme:
Puis sera l'vn esleu de mesme temps,
Qui des Romains ne sera trop conforme.

Quatrain 5,93

Soubs le terroir du rond globe lunaire,
Lors que sera dominateur Mercure:
L'isle d'Escosse fera vn luminaire,
Qui les Anglois mettra à deconfiture.

Quatrain 5,96

Sur le milieu du grand monde la rose,
Pour nouueaux faicts sang public espandu:
A dire vray on aura bouche close,
Lors au besoing viendra tard l'attendu.

Quatrain 5,98

A quarante huict degré climaterique,
A fin de Cancer si grande seicheresse:
Poisson en mer, fleuue: lac cuit hectique,
Bearn, Bigorre par feu ciel en detresse.

CENTURIE VI

Quatrain 6,2

En l'an cinq cens octante plus & moins,
On attendra le siecle bien estrange:
En l'an sept cens, & trois cieux en tesmoings,
Que plusieurs regnes vn à cinq feront change.

Quatrain 6,3

Fleuue qu'esprouue le nouueau nay de Celtique
Sera en grande de l'Empire discordes
Le ieune prince par gent ecclesiastique,
Ostera le sceptre coronal de concorde.

Quatrain 6,4

La Celtiq fleuue changera de riuage,
Plus ne tiendra la cité d'Agripine:
Tout transmué hormis le vieil langage,
Saturne, Leo, Mars, Cancer en rapine.

Quatrain 6,5

Si grand famine par vnde pestifere.
Par pluye longue le long du polle arctiques
Samatobryn cent lieux de l'hemisphere,
Viuront sans loy exempt de pollitique.

Quatrain 6,7

Norneigre Dace, & l'Isle Britannique,
Par les vnis freres seront vexees:
Le chef Romain issu de sang Gallique
Et les copies aux forests repoussees.

Quatrain 6,8

Ceux qui estoient en regne pour s'accedeauoir,
Au Royal change deuiendront appouuris:
Vns exilez sans appuy or n'auoir,
Lettrez & lettres ne seront à grand pris.

Quatrain 6,9

Aux sacrez temples seront faicts escandales,
Comptez seront par honneurs & loüanges:
D'vn que on graue d'argent d'or les medalles,
La fin sera en tourmens bien estranges.

Quatrain 6,10

Vn peu de temps les temples des couleurs
De blanc & noir des deux entre meslee:
Rouges & iaunes leur embleront les leurs,
Sang, terre, peste, faim, feu d'eau affollee.

Quatrain 6,11

Des sept rameaux à trois seront reduicts,
Les plus aisnez seront surprins par mort,
Fratricider les deux seront seduicts,
Les coniurez en dormans seront morts.

Quatrain 6,12

Dresser copies pour monter à l'empire,
Du Vatican le sang Royal tiendra:
Flamans, Anglois, Espagne auec Aspire,
Contre l'Italie & France contiendra.

Quatrain 6,13

Par les Phisiques le grand Roy delaissé,
Par sort non art de l'Ebrieu est en vie,
Luy & son genre au regne haut poussé,
Grace donnee à gent qui Christ enuie.

Quatrain 6,19

La vraye flamme engloutira la dame,
Qui voudra mettre les Innocens à feu:
Pres de l'assaut l'exercite s'enflamme,
Quant dans Seuille monstre en boeuf sera veu.

Quatrain 6,20

L'vnion feincte sera peu de duree,
Des vn changez reformez la pluspart:
Dans les vaisseaux sera gent endurees,
Lors aura Rome vn nouueau Liepart.

Quatrain 6,21

Quant ceux du polle arctic vnis ensemble,
Et Orient grand effrayeur & craints:
Esleu nouueau, soustenu le grand tremble,
Rodes, Bisence de sang Barbare teincte.

Quatrain 6,22

Dedans la terre du grand temple celique,
Nepueu à Londre par paix feincte meurtry:
La barque alors deuiendra scimatique,
Liberté feincte sera au corn' & cry.

Quatrain 6,23

D'esprit de regne munismes descriés,
Et seront peuples esmeuz contre leur Roy,
Paix sainct nouueau, sainctes loix empirees,
Rapis onc fut en si tredur arroy.

Quatrain 6,24

Mars & le scepte se trouuera conioinct,
Dessoubs Cancer calamiteuse guerre:
Vn peu apres sera nouueau Roy oingt,
Qui par long temps pacifiera la terre.

Quatrain 6,25

Dedans les Isles de cinq fleuues à vn,
Par le croissant du grand Chyren Selin:
Par les bruynes de l'air fureur de l'vn,
Six eschapez cachez fardeaux de lyn.

Quatrain 6,31

Roy trouuera ce qu'il desiroit tant,
Quand le Prelat sera reprins à tort:
Responce au Duc le rendra mal content,
Qui dans Milan mettra plusieurs à mort.

Quatrain 6,32

Par trahison de verges à mort battu,
Prins surmonté sera par son desordre:
Conseil friuole au grand captif sentu,
Nez par fureur quant Berlch viendra mordre.

Quatrain 6,33

Sa main derniere par Alus sanguinaire,
Ne se pourra par la mer garentir:
Entre deux fleuues craindre main militaire,
Le noir l'ireux le fera repentir.

Quatrain 6,34

De feu voulant la machination,
Viendra troubler au grand chef assieger:
Dedans sera telle sedition,
Qu'en desespoir seront les profligez.

Quatrain 6,37

L'oeuure ancienne se paracheuera,
Du toict cherra sur le grand mal ruyne:
Innocent faict mort on accusera,
Nocent cache, taillis à la bruyne.

Quatrain 6,38

Aux profligez de paix les ennemis,
Apres auoir l'Italie superee,
Noir sanguinaire, rouge. sera commis,
Feu, sang verser, eau de sang coloree.

Quatrain 6,41

Le second chef du regne d'Annemarc,
Par ceux de Frize & l'Isle Britannique,
Fera despendre plus de cent mille marc,
Vain exploicter voyage en Italique.

Quatrain 6,42

A Logmyon sera laissé le regne,
Du grand Selin plus fera de faict:
Par les Itales estendra son enseigne,
Regi sera par prudent contrefaict.

Quatrain 6,43

Long temps sera sans estre habitee,
Où Signe & Marne autour vient arrouser:
De la Tamise & martiaux tentee,
De ceux les gardes en cuidant repousser.

Quatrain 6,44

De nuict par Nantes Lyris apparoistra,
Des arts marins susciteront la pluye:
Vrabiq goulfre, grande classe parfondra,
Vn monstre en Saxe naistra d'ours & truye.

Quatrain 6,46

Vn iuste sera en exil renuoyé,
Par pestilence aux confins de Nonseggle,
Response au rouge le fera desuoyé,
Roy retirant à la Rame & à l'Aigle.

Quatrain 6,47

Entre deux monts les deux grands assemblez.
Delaisseront leur simulté secrette:
Brucelle & Dolle par Langres accablez,
Pour à Malignes executeur leur peste.

Quatrain 6,49

De la partie de Mammer grand Pontife,
Subiuguera les confins du Danube:
Chasser la croix, par ter ratté ne ritfe,
Captifs, or, bague plus de cent mille rubes.

Quatrain 6,50

Dedans le puys seront trouuez les os,
Sera l'inceste, commis par la maratre:
L'estat changé, on querra bruit & los,
Et aura Mars atrendant pour son astre.

Quatrain 6,51

Peuple assemblé, voir nouueau expectacle.
Princes & Roys par plusieurs assistans,
Pilliers faillir, murs: mais comme miracle
Le Roy sauué & trente des instans.

Quatrain 6,52

En lieu du grand qui sera condamné,
De prison hors, son amy en sa place:
L'espoir Troyen en six mois ioins, mort né,
Le Sol à l'vrne seront peins fleuue en glace.

Quatrain 6,53

Le grand Prelat Celtique à Roy suspect,
De nuict par cours sortira hors de regne:
Par Duc fertile à son grand Roy Bretaine,
Bisance à Cypres & Tunes insuspect.

Quatrain 6,54

Au poinct du iour au second chant du coq,
Ceux de Tunes, de Fez, & de Bugie,
Par les Arabes, captif le Roy Maroq,
L'an mil six cens & sept, de Liturgie.

Quatrain 6,56

La crainte armee de l'ennemy Narbon
Effrayera si fort les Hesperidues:
Parpignan vuide par l'aueugle d'arbon,
Lors Barcelon par mer donra les piques.

Quatrain 6,57

Celui qu'estoit bien auant dans le regne,
Ayant chef rouge proche à hierarchie,
Aspre & cruel, & se fera tant craindre,
Succedera à sacré monarchie.

Quatrain 6,58

Entre les deux monarques esloignez,
Lors que le Sol par Selin clair perduë,
Simulté grande entre deux indignez,
Qu'aux Isles & Sienne la liberte renduë.

Quatrain 6,60

Le Prince hors de son terroir Celtique
Sera trahy, deceu par interprete:
Roüant, Rochelle par ceux de l'Armorique
Au port de Blaue deceus par moyne & prestre.

Quatrain 6,61

Le grand tappis plié ne monstrera,
Fors qu'à demy la pluspart de l'histoire:
Chassé du regne loing aspre apparoistra,
Qu'au faict bellique chacun le viendra croire.

Quatrain 6,63

La dame seule au regne demeuree.
D'vnic esteint premier au lict d'honneur:
Sept ans sera de douleur exploree,
Puis longue vie au regne par grand, heur.

Quatrain 6,66

Au fondement de la nouuelle secte,
Seront les os du grand Romain trouuez,
Sepulchre en marbre apparoistra couuerte,
Terre trembler en Auril, mal enfoüetz.

Quatrain 6,70

Au chef du monde le grand Chyren sera,
Plus outre apres ayme, criant, redouté:
Son bruit & los les cieux surpassera,
Et du seul tiltre victeur fort contenté.

Quatrain 6,72

Par fureur feinte d'esmotion diuine,
Sera la femme du grand fort violee:
Iuges voulans damner telle doctrine,
Victime au peuple ignorant immolee.

Quatrain 6,74

La dechassee au regne tournera,
Ses ennemis trouuez des coniurez:
Plus que iamais son temps triomphera,
Trois & septante à mort trop asseurez.

Quatrain 6,77

Par la victoire du deceu fraudulente,
Deux classes vne, la reuolte Germanie,
Le chef meurtry & son fils dans la tente,
Florence, Imole pourchassez dans Romaine.

Quatrain 6,78

Crier victoire du grand Selin croissant:
Par les Romains sera l'Aigle clamé,
Tiecin Millan et Genes y consent,
Puis par eux mesmes Basil grand reclamé.

Quatrain 6,80

De Fez le regne paruiendra à ceux d'Europe,
Feu leur cité & l'anne tranchera.
Le grand d'Asie terre & mer à grand troupe,
Que bleux, peres, croix, à mort dechassera.

Quatrain 6,81

Pleurs cris & plaints heurlemens, effrayeur,
Coeur inhumain, cruel, Roy & transy.
Leman les Isles, de Gennes les maieurs,
Sang espacher, fromfaim à nul mercy.

Quatrain 6,82

Par les deserts de lieu libre & farouche,
Viendra errer nepueu du grand Pontife:
Assommé à sept auecques lourde souche,
Par ceux qu'apres occuperont le Cyphe.

Quatrain 6,84

Celuy qu'en Sparte Claude ne peut regner,
Il fera tant par voye seductiue:
Que du court, long, le fera araigner,
Que contre Roy fera sa perspectiue.

Quatrain 6,86

Le grand Prelat vn iour apres son songe,
Interpreté au rebours de son sens:
De la Gascogne luy suruiendra vn monge,
Qui fera eslire le grand prelat de Sens.

Quatrain 6,87

L'election faicte dans Frankfort,
N'aura nul lieu, Milan s'opposera:
Le sien plus proche semblera si grand fort,
Qu'outre le Rhin és mareschs cassera.

Quatrain 6,88

Vn regne grand demourra desolé,
Aupres de l'Hebro se feront assemblees:
Monts Pyrenees le rendront consolé,
Lors que dans May seront terres tremblees.

Quatrain 6,89

Entre deux cymbes pieds & mains attachez,
De miel face oingt, & de laict substanté,
Guespes & mouchez, fitine amour fachez
Poccilateur faucer, Cyphe tenté.

Quatrain 6,90

L'honnissement puant abominable
Apres le faict sera felicité
Grand excuse pour n'estre fauorable,
Qu'à paix Neptune ne sera incité.

Quatrain 6,91

Grande cité à soldats abandonnee,
On n'y eu mortel tumult si proche:
O qu'elle hideuse mortalité s'approche,
Fors vne offence n'y sera pardonnee.

Quatrain 6,92

Cinq & quarante degrez ciel bruslera
Feu approcher de la grand cité neuue
Instant grand flamme esparse sautera
Quand on voudra des Normans faire preuue.

Quatrain 6,99

L'ennemy docte se trouuera confus.
Grand camp malade, & defaict par embusches,
Môts Pyrenees & Poenus luy serôt faicts refus,
Proche du fleuue descouurant antiques roches.

LEGIS CANTIO CONTRA INEPTOS CRITICOS

Quos legent hosce versus maturè censunto,
Profanum vulgus & inscium ne attrectato:
Omnesq; Astrologi, Blennis, Barbari procul sunto,
Qui aliter facit, is rite sacer esto.

CENTVRIE VII

Quatrain 7,3

Apres de France la victoire navale,
Les Barchinons, Saillinons, les Phocens,
Lierre d'or, l'enclume serré dedans la basle,
Ceux de Ptolon au fraud seront consens.

Quatrain 7,5

Vin sur la table en sera respandu
Le tiers n'aura celle qu'il pretendoit:
Deux fois du noir de Parme descendu,
Perouse à Pize fera ce qu'il cuidoit.

Quatrain 7,11

L'enfant Royal contemnera la mere,
Oeil, piedz blessés, rude, inobeissant,
Nouvelle à dame estrange & bien amere,
Seront tués des siens plus de cinq cens.

Quatrain 7,13

De la cité marine & tributaire,
La teste raze prendra la satrapie:
Chasser sordide qui puis sera contraire
Par quatorze ans tiendra la tyrannie.

Quatrain 7,22

Les citoyens de Mesopotamie,
Yreés encontre amis de Tarraconne,
Jeux, ritz, banquetz, toute gent endormie
Vicaire au Rosne, prins cité, ceux d'Ausone.

Quatrain 7,24

L'enseveli sortira du tombeau,
Fera de chaines lier le fort du pont:
Empoisonné avec oeufz de Barbeau,
Grand de Lorraine par le Marquis du Pont.

Quatrain 7,25

Par guerre longue tout l'exercite expulser,
Que pour souldartz ne trouveront pecune:
Lieu d'or d'argent, cuir on viendra cuser,
Gualois aerain, signe croissant de Lune.

Quatrain 7,28

Le capitaine conduira grande proie,
Sur la montaigne des ennemis plus proche,
Environné, par feu fera tel voie,
Tous eschappez or trente mis en broche.

Quatrain 7,30

Le sac s'approche, feu, grand sang espandu
Po, grand fleuves, aux bouviers l'entreprinse,
De Gennes, Nice, apres long attendu,
Foussan, Turin, à Savillon la prinse.

Quatrain 7,32

Du mont Royal naistra d'une casane,
Qui cave, & compte viendra tyranniser
Dresser copie de la marche Millane,
Favene, Florence d'or & gens espuiser.

Quatrain 7,33

Par frause regne, forces expolier,
La classe obsesse, passages à l'espie:
Deux fainctz amis se viendront rallier,
Esveiller haine de long temps assoupie.

Quatrain 7,34

En grand regret sera la gent Gauloise
Coeur vain, legier croirera temerité:
Pain, sel, ne vin, eaue : venin ne cervoise
Plus grand captif, faim, froid, necessité.

Quatrain 7,35

La grand pesche viendra plaindre, plorer
D'avoir esleu, trompés seront en l'aage:
Guiere avec eux ne voudra demourer,
Deçue sera par ceux de son langaige.

Quatrain 7,36

Dieu, le ciel tout le divin verbe à l'unde,
Porté par rouger sept razes à Bisance:
Contre les oingz trois cens de Trebisconde,
Deux loix mettront, & l'horreur, puis credence.

Quatrain 7,40

Dedans tonneaux hors oingz d'huile & gresse,
Seront vingt un devant le port fermés,
Au second guet par mont feront prouesse:
Gaigner les portes & du guet assommés.

Quatrain 7,42

Deux de poison saisiz nouveau venuz,
Dans la cuisine du grand Prince verser:
Par le soillard tous deux au faicts cogneuz
Prins que cuidoit de mort l'aisné vexer.

CENTVRIE VIII

Quatrain 8,1

PAU, NAY, LORON plus feu qu'à sang sera.
Laude nager, fuir grand au surrez.
Les agassas entree refusera.
Pampon, Durancde les tiendra enferrez.

Quatrain 8,5

Apparoistra temple luisant orné,
La lampe & cierge à Borne & Bretueil.
Pour la lucerne le canton destorné,
Quand on verra le grand coq au cercueil.

Quatrain 8,10

Puanteur grande sortira de Lausanne,
Qu'on ne seura l'origine du fait,
Lon mettra hors toute le gente loingtaine
Feu veu au ciel, peuple estranger deffait.

Quatrain 8,13

Le croisé frere par amour effréné
Fera par Praytus Bellesophon mourir,
Classe à mil ans la femme forcenée,
Beu le breuvage, tous deux apres perir.

Quatrain 8,14

Le grand credit d'or, d'argent l'abondance
Fera aveugler par libide honneur
Sera cogneu d'adultere l'offense,
Qui parviendra à son grand deshonneur.

Quatrain 8,15

Vers Aquilon grans efforts par hommasse
Presque l'Europe & l'univers vexer,
Les deux eclipse mettra en tel chasse,
Et aux Pannons vie & mort renforcer.

Quatrain 8,16

Au lieu que HIERON feit sa nef fabriquer,
Si grand deluge sera & si subite,
Qu'on n'aura lieu ne terres s'atacquer
L'onde monter Fesulan Olympique.

Quatrain 8,17

Les bien aisez subit seront desmis
Par les trois freres le monde mis en trouble,
Cité marine saisiront ennemis,
Faim, feu, sang, peste & de tous maux le double.

Quatrain 8,20

Le faux messaige par election fainte
Courir par urban rompu pache arreste,
Voix acheptees, de sang chappelle tainte,
Et à un autre l'empire contraicte.

Quatrain 8,21

Au port d'Agde trois fustes entreront
Portant d'infect non foi & pestilence
Passant le pont mil milles embleront,
Et le pont rompre à tierce resistance.

Quatrain 8,23

Lettres trouvées de la roine les coffres,
Point de subscrit sans aucun nom d'hauteur
Par la police seront caché les offres.
Qu'on ne scaura qui sera l'amateur.

Quatrain 8,25

Coeur de l'amant ouvert d'amour fertive
Dans le ruisseau fera ravir la Dame,
Le demi mal contrefera lassive,
Le père à deux privera corps de l'ame.

Quatrain 8,28

Les simulacres d'or & argent enflez,
Qu'apres le rapt au lac furent gettez
Au desouvert estaincts tous & troublez.
Au marbre script prescript intergetez.

Quatrain 8,29

Au quart pillier l'on sacre à Saturne.
Par tremblant terre & deluge fendu
Soubz l'edifice Saturnin trouvee urne,
D'or Capion ravi & puis rendu.

Quatrain 8,31

Premier grand fruit le prince de Perquiere
Mais puis viendra bien & cruel malin,
Dedans Venise perdra sa gloire fiere
Et mis à mal par plus joune Celin.

Quatrain 8,32

Garde toi roi Gaulois de ton nepveu
Qui fera tant que ton unique fils
Sera meutri à Venus faisant voeu,
Accompaigné de nuit que trois & six.

Quatrain 8,37

La forteresse aupres de la Tamise
Cherra par lors le Roi dedans serré,
Aupres du pont sera veu en chemise
Un devant mort, puis dans le fort barré.

Quatrain 8,41

Esleu sera Renad ne sonnant mot,
Faisant le saint public vivant pain d'orge,
Tyranniser apres tant à un cop,
Mettant à pied des plus grans sus la gorge.

Quatrain 8,43

Par le decide de deux choses bastars
Nepveu du sang occupera le regne
Dedans lectoyre seront les coups de dars
Nepveu par peur plaire l'enseigne.

Quatrain 8,44

Le procreé naturel d'ogmion,
De sept à neuf du Chemin destorner
A roi de longue & ami au mi-hom,
Doit à Navarre fort de PAU prosterner.

Quatrain 8,48

Saturne en Cancer, Jupiter avec Mars,
Dedans Feurier Chaldondon salvaterre.
Sault Castalon affailli de trois pars,
Pres de Verbiesque conflit mortelle guerre.

Quatrain 8,54

Soubz la colleur du traicte mariage,
Fait magnamine par grand Chyren selin.
Quintin, Arras recouvres au voyage
D'espaignolz fait second banc macelin.

Quatrain 8,55

Entre deux fleuves se verra enserré,
Tonneaux & caques unis à passer outre,
Huict poutz rompus chef à tant enferré,
Enfans parfaictz sont jugetez en coultre.

Quatrain 8,58

Regne en querelle aux freres divisé,
Prendre les armes & le nom Britannique
Tiltre Anglican sera guard advisé,
Surprins de nuict mener à l'air Gallique.

Quatrain 8,59

Par deux fois hault, par deux fois mis à bas
L'orient aussie l'occident faiblira
Son adversaire apres plusiers combats,
Par mer chassé au besoin faillira.

Quatrain 8,60

Premier en Gaule, premier en Romanie
Par mer & terre aux Anglois & Paris
Merveilleux faitz par celle grand mesnie
Violent terax perdra le NORLARIS.

Quatrain 8,66

Quand l'escritue D.M. trouvee,
En cave antique à lampe descouverte,
Loi, Roi, & Prince Ulpian esprouvee
Pavillon rogne & Duc sous la couvert.

Quatrain 8,69

Aupres du jeune le vieux ange baisser
Et le viendra surmonter à la fin:
Dix ans esgaux au plus vieux rabaisser,
De trois deux l'un huitiesme seraphin.

Quatrain 8,70

Il entrera vilain, mechant, infame
Tyrannisant la Mesopotamie,
Tous amis fait d'adulterine d'ame,
Terre horrible, noir de phisonomie.

Quatrain 8,71

Croistra le nombre si grand des astronomes
Chassez, bannis & livres consurez,
L'an mil six cents sept par sacre glomes
Que nul aux sacres ne seront asseurez.

Quatrain 8,73

Soldat barbare le grand Roi frappera,
Injustement non esloigné de mort,
L'avare mere du fait cause fera
Conjurateur & regne en grand remort.

Quatrain 8,74

En terre neufue bien avant Roi entré
Pendant subges lui viendront faire acueil,
Sa perfidie aura tel recontré
Qu'aux citadins lieu de feste & receuil.

Quatrain 8,75

Le pere & fils seront meurdris ensemble
Le prefecteur dedans son pavillon
La mere à Tours du filz ventre aura enfle
Criche verdure de failles papillon.

Quatrain 8,76

Plus Macelin que roi en Angleterre
Lieu obscure nay par force aura l'empire:
Lasche sans foi, sans loi saignera terre,
Son temps approche si presque je soupire.

Quatrain 8,77

L'antechrist trois bien tost anniehilez,
Vingt & sept ans sang durera sa guerre.
Les heretiques mortz, captifs, exilez.
Sang corps humain eau rougi gresler terre.

Quatrain 8,78

Un Bragamus avec la langue torte
Viendra des dieux le sanctuaire,
Aux heretiques il ouvrira la porte
En suscitant l'eglise militaire.

Quatrain 8,79

Qui par fer pere perdra nay de Nonnaire,
De Gorgon sur la sera sang perfetant
En terre estrange fera si tant de taire,
Qui bruslera lui mesme & son enfant.

Quatrain 8,80

Des innocens le sang de vefue & vierge.
Tant de maulx faitz par moyen se grand Roge
Saintz simulacres tremper en ardent cierge
De frayeur crainte ne verra nul que boge.

Quatrain 8,81

Le neuf empire en desolation
Sera changé du pole aquilonaire.
De la Sicile viendra l'esmotion
Troubler l'emprise à Philip tributaire.

Quatrain 8,87

Mort conspiree viendra en plein effect,
Charge donnee & voiage de mort,
Esleu, crée, receu par siens deffait.
Sang d'innocence devant foi par remort.

Quatrain 8,90

Quand des croisez un trouvé de sens trouble
En lieu du sacre verra un boeuf cornu
Par vierge porc son lieu lors sera comble
Par roi plus ordre ne sera soustenu.

Quatrain 8,95

Le seducteur sera mis en la fosse
Et estaché jusques à quelque temps,
Le clerc uni le chef avec sa crosse
Picante droite attraira les contens.

Quatrain 8,96

La synagogue sterile sans nul fruit
Sera receu entre les infideles
De Babylon la fille du porsuit
Misere & triste lui trenchera les aisles.

Quatrain 8,97

A fin du VAR changer le pompotans,
Pres du rivage les trois beaux enfants naistre.
Ruine ay peuple par aage competans.
Regne ay pays changer plus voir croistre.

Quatrain 8,100

Pour l'abondance de larme respandue
Du hault en bas par le bas au plus hault.
Trop grande foir par jeu vie perdue
De soif mourir par habondant deffault.

CENTVRIE IX

Quatrain 9,1

Dans la maison du traducteur de Bourç
Seront les lettres trouuees sur la table,
Borgne, roux, blanç chanu tiendra de cours,
Qui changera au nouueau Connestable.

Quatrain 9,6

Par la Guyenne infinité d'Anglois
Occuperont par nom d'Anglaquitaine,
Du Languedoc Ispalme Bourdeloys,
Qu'ils nommeront apres Barboxitaine.

Quatrain 9,7

Qui ouurira le monument trouué,
Et ne viendra le serrer promptement,
Mal luy viendra, & ne pourra prouué
Si mieux doit estre Roy Breton ou Normand.

Quatrain 9,8

Puisnay Roy fait son père mettre à mort,
Apres conflict de mort tres-inhonneste:
Escrit trouué, soupçon donna remort,
Quand loup chassé pose sur la couchette.

Quatrain 9,9

Quand lampe ardente de feu inextinguible
Sera trouué au temple des Vestales.
Enfant trouué feu, eau passant par crible:
Perir eau Nymes, Tholose cheoir les halles.

Quatrain 9,14

Mis en planure chauderons d'infecteurs,
Vin, miel & huyle & bastis sur fourneauxs
Seront plongez, sans mal dit malfacteurs
Sept fum extaint au canon des bordeaux.

Quatrain 9,16

De castel Franco sortira l'assemblee,
L'ambassadeur non plaisant fera scisme:
Ceux de Ribiere seront en la meslee,
Et au grand goulfre desnie ont l'entree.

Quatrain 9,17

Le tiers premier pis que ne fit Neron,
Vuidez vaillant que sang humain respandre:
Rédifier fera le forneron,
Siecle d'or mort, nouueau Roy grâd esclandre.

Quatrain 9,27

De bois la garde, vent clos ronds pont sera,
Haut le receu frappera le Dauphin,
Le vieux teccon bois vnis passera,
Passant plus outre du Duc le droit confin.

Quatrain 9,31

Le tremblement de terre à Morrura,
Caffich sainct George à demy perfondrez:
Paix assoupie la guerre esueillera,
Dans temple à Pasques abysmes enfondrez.

Quatrain 9,32

De fin porphire profond collon trouuee
Dessouz la laze escripts capitolin:
Os poil retors Romain force prouuee,
Classe agiter au port de Methelin.

Quatrain 9,33

Hercules Roy de Rome & d'Annemarç
De Gaule trois Guion surnommé,
Trembler l'Italie & l'vnde de sainct Març
Premier sur tous monarque renommé.

Quatrain 9,36

Vn grând Roy prins entre les mains d'vn Ioyne,
Non loin de Pasque confusion coup cultre:
Perpet, captifs foudre en la husne,
Lors que trois freres se blesseront & murtre.

Quatrain 9,37

Pont & moulins en Decembre versez,
En si haut lieu montera la Garonne:
Meurs, edifices, Tolose renuersez,
Qu'on ne sçaura son lieu autant matronne.

Quatrain 9,41

Le grand Chyren soy saisir d'Auignon,
De Rome lettres en miel plein d'amertu
Lettre ambassade partir de Chanignon,
Carpentras pris par duc noir rouge plum

Quatrain 9,43

Proche à descendre l'armee Crucigere,
Sera guettee par les Ismae"lites,
De tous costez batus par nef Rauiere,
Prompt assaillis de dix galeres eslites.

Quatrain 9,44

Migrés, migrés de Geneue trestous.
Saturne d'or en fer se changera,
Le contre FAYPOZ exterminera tous,
Auant l'aduent le ciel signes fera.

Quatrain 9,45

Ne sera soul iamais de demander,
Grand Mendosus obtiendra son empire:
Loing de la cour fera contremander
Pymond, Picard, Paris Tyrron le pire.

Quatrain 9,46

Vuydez fuyez de Tolose les ronges,
Du sacrifice faire piation.
Le chef du mal dessous l'ombre des courges:
Mort estrangler carne omination.

Quatrain 9,48

La grand cité d'Occean maritime,
Enuironnee de marets en cristal:
Dans le solstice hyemal & la prime,
Sera tentee de vent espouuantal.

Quatrain 9,50

Mandosus tost viendra à son haut regne,
Mettant arriere vn peu les Norlaris:
Le rouge blesme, le masle a l'interregne,
Le ieune crainte & frayeur Barbaris.

Quatrain 9,51

Contre les rouges sectes se banderont,
Feu, eau, fer, corde par paix se minera:
An point mourir ceux qui machineront,
Fors vn que monde sur tout ruinera.

Quatrain 9,52

La paix s'approche d'vn costé, & la guerre,
Oncques ne fut la poursuitte si grande:
Plaindre hômme, femme sang innocent par terre,
Et ce sera de France a toute bande.

Quatrain 9,53

Le Neron ieune dans le trois cheminees,
Fera de paiges vifs pour ardoir ietter:
Heureux qui loing sera de tels menees,
Trois de son sang le feront mort guetter.

Quatrain 9,57

Au lieu de DRVX vn Roy reposera,
Et cherchera loy changeant d'Anatheme:
Pendant le ciel si tresfort tonnera,
Portera neufue Roy tuera soy mesme.

Quatrain 9,60

Conflict Barbar en la Cornette noire,
Sang espandu, trembler la Dalmatie:
Grand Ismael mettra son promontoire,
Ranes trembler secours Lusitanie.

Quatrain 9,62

Au grand de Chera mon agora,
Seront croisez par ranc tous attachez,
Le pertinax Oppi, & Mandragora,
Raugon d'Octobre le tiers seront laschez.

Quatrain 9,63

Plainctes & pleurs cris, & grands hurlemens
Pres de Narbon a Bayonne & en Foix,
O quels horribles calamitez changemens,
Auant que Mars reuolu quelquefois.

Quatrain 9,65

Dedans le coing de Luna viendra rendre
Où sera prins & mis en terre estrange.
Les fruicts immeurs seront à grand esclandre,
Grand vitupere, à l'vn grande lou"ange.

Quatrain 9,66

Paix, vnion sera & changement,
Estats, offices bas haut & haut bien bas
Dresser voyage, le fruict premier tourment,
Guerre cesser, ciuil proces debats.

Quatrain 9,68

Du mont Aymar sera noble obscurcie,
Le mal viendra au ioinct de Saone & Rosne:
Dans bois cachez soldats iour de Lucie
Qui ne fut onc vn si horrible throsne.

Quatrain 9,71

Aux lieux sacrez animaux veu à trixe,
Auec celuy qui n'osera le iour.
A Carcassonne pour disgrace propice,
Sera posé pour plus amule seiour.

Quatrain 9,73

Dans Fois entrez Roy ceiulee Turban:
Et regnera moins euolu Saturne,
Roy Turban blanc Bizance coeur ban,
Sol, Mars, Mercure pres la hurne.

Quatrain 9,74

Dans la cité de Fertsod homicide,
Fait, & fait multe beuf arant ne macter,
Retours encores aux honneurs d'Artemide
Et à Vulcan corps morts sepulturer.

Quatrain 9,77

Le regne prins le Roy coniurera
La dame prinse à mort iurez à sort,
La vie à Royne fils on desniera,
Et la pellix au fort de la consort.

Quatrain 9,78

La dame Grecque de beauté laydique,
Heureuse faicte de procs innumerable,
Hors translatee en regne Hispanique,
Captiue prinse mourir mort miserable.

Quatrain 9,80

Le Duc voudra les siens exterminer,
Enuoyera les plus forts lieux estranges:
Par tyrannie Bize & Luc ruiner,
Puy les Barbares sans vin feront vendanges.

Quatrain 9,81

Le Roy rusé entendra ses embusches,
De trois quartiers ennemis assaillir:
Vn nombre estrange larmes de coqueluches,
Viendra Lemprin du traducteur faillir.

Quatrain 9,83

Sol vingt de Taurus si fort de terre trembler,
Le grand theatre remply ruinera:
L'air, ciel & terre obscurcir & troubler,
Lors l'infidelle Dieu & saincts voguera.

Quatrain 9,84

Roy exposé parfera l'hecatombe,
Apres auoir trouué son origine:
Torrent ouurir de marbre & plomb la tombe,
D'vn grand Romain d'enseigne Medusine.
People who would end the rout deterred.

Quatrain 9,89

Sept ans sera Philipp. fortune prospere.
Rabaissera des Arabes l'effort,
Puis son midy perplex rebors affaire,
Ieune ognion abismera son fort.

Quatrain 9,90

Vn capitaine de la Grand Germanie
Se viendra rendre par simulé secours
Au Roy des Roys aide de Pannoie,
Que sa reuolte fera de sang grand cours.

Quatrain 9,92

Le Roy voudra en cité neufue entrer,
Par ennemis expugner l'on viendra
Captif libere faux dire & perpetrer,
Roy dehors estre, loin d'ennemis tiendra.

Quatrain 9,94

Foibles galeres seront vnies ensemble,
Ennemis faux le plus fort en rampart:
Foibles assaillies Vratislaue tremble,
Lubecq & Mysne tiendront barbare part.

Quatrain 9,98

Les affigez par faute d'vn seul taint,
Contremenant à partie opposite,
Aux Lygonnois mandera que contraint
Seront de rendre le grand chef de Molite.

Quatrain 9,100

Naualle pugne nuit sera superee.
Le feu aux naues à l'Occident ruine:
Rubriche neufue, la grand nef coloree,
Ire à vaincu, & victoire en bruine.

CENTVRIE X

Quatrain 10,1

A L'ennemy, l'ennemy foy promise
Ne se tiendra, les captifs retenus:
Prins preme mort, & le reste en chemise.
Damné le reste pour estre soustenus.

Quatrain 10,3

En apres cinq troupeau ne mettra hors vn
Fuitif pour Penelon laschera,
Faux murmurer, secours vnir pour lors,
Le chef le siege pour lors abandonnera.

Quatrain 10,4

Sur la minuict conducteur de l'armee
Se sauuera subit esuanouy,
Sept ans apres la fame non blasmee,
A son retour ne dira onc ouy.

Quatrain 10,7

Le grand conflit qu'on appreste à Nancy,
L'Aemathien dira tout ie soubmets,
L'Isle Britanne par vin sel en solcy:
Hem, mi. deux Phi. long temps ne tiêdra Mets.

Quatrain 10,8

Index & poulse parfondera le front,
De Senegalia le Conte à son fils propre,
La Myrnamee par plusieurs de prin front,
Trois dans sept iours blessés mort.

Quatrain 10,10

Tasche de meurdre, enormes adulteres,
Grand ennemy de tout le genre humain:
Que sera pire qu'ayeuls, oncles ne peres,
En fer, feu, eaux, sanguin & inhumain.

Quatrain 10,12

Esleu en Pape, d'esleu se mocqué,
Subit soudain esmeu prompt & timide,
Par trop bon doux à mourrir prouoqué,
Crainte esteinte la nuict de sara mort guide.

Quatrain 10,13

Souz la pasture d'animaux ruminant,
Par eux conduicts au ventre helbipolique,
Soldats cachez, les armes bruit menant,
Non long temptez de cité Antipolique.

Quatrain 10,14

Vrnel Vaucile sans conseil de soy mesmes,
Hardit timide, car crainte prins vaincu,
Accompagné de plusieurs putains blesmes.
A Barcellonne au Chartreux conuaincu.

Quatrain 10,15

Pere duc vieux d'ans & de soif chargé,
Au iour extreme fils desniant l'esguiere.
Dedans le puits vif mort viendra plongé.
Senat au fil la mort longue & legere.

Quatrain 10,20

Tous les amis qu'auront tenu party,
Pour rude en lettres mis mort & saccagé
Biens publiez par fixe grand neanty,
Onc Romain peuple ne fut tant outragé.

Quatrain 10,21

Par le despit du Roy soustenant moindre,
Sera meurdry luy presentant les bagues:
Le pere au fils voulant noblesse poindre,
Fait comme à Perse jadis firent les Magues.

Quatrain 10,22

Pour ne vouloir consentir au diuorce,
Qui puis apres sera cogneu indigne:
Le Roy des isles sera chassé par sorte,
Mais à son lieu qui de roy n'aura signe.

Quatrain 10,24

Le captif prince aux Itales vaincu
Passera Gennes par mer iusqu'à Marceille,
Par grand effort des forens suruaincu
Sauf coup de feu barril liqueur d'abeille.

Quatrain 10,25

Par Nebro ouurir de Bisanne passage,
Bien esloignez el tago fara moestra,
Dans Pelligouxe sera commis l'outrage,
De la grand dame assise sur l'orchestra

Quatrain 10,26

Le successeur vengera son beau frere,
Occuper regne souz vmbre de vengeance,
Occis ostacle son sang mort vitupere,
Long temps Bretaigne tiendra auec la France.

Quatrain 10,27

Par le cinquiesme & vn grand Hercules
Viendront le temple ouurir de main bellique,
Vn Clement, Iule & Ascans recules,
L'espee, clef, aigle, n'eurent onc si grand picque.

Quatrain 10,30

Nepveu & sang du sainct nouueau venu,
Par le surnom soustient arcs & couuert
Seront chassez mis à mort chassez nu,
En rouge & noir conuertiront leur vert.

Quatrain 10,31

Le sainct Empire, viendra en Germanie
Ismaëlites trouueront lieux ouuerts,
Asnes voudront aussi la Carmanie
Les soustenans de terre tous couuerts.

Quatrain 10,32

Le grand empire chacun an deuoit estre,
Vn sur les autres le viendra obtenir:
Mais peu de temps sera son reigne & estre,
Deux ans naues se pourra soustenir.

Quatrain 10,33

La faction cruelle à robe longue,
Viendra cacher souz ses pointus poignards,
Saisir Florence le Duc & lieu diphlonque,
Sa descouuerte par immurs & flangnards.

Quatrain 10,35

Puisnay royal flagrant d'ardant libide,
Pour se iouyr de cousine germaine:
Habit de femme au temple d'Arthemide,
Allant meurdry par incognu du Maine.

Quatrain 10,36

Apres le Roy du soucq guerres parlant,
L'Isle Harmotique le tiendra à mespris:
Quelques ans bons rongeant vn & pillant,
Par tyrannie à l'isle changeant pris.

Quatrain 10,38

Amour allegre non loing pose le siege.
Au sainct barbar seront les garnisons:
Vrsins Hadrie pour Gaulois feront plaige,
Pour peur rendus de l'armee aux Grisons.

Quatrain 10,40

Le ieune n'ay au regne Britannique,
Qu'aura le pere mourant recommandé,
Iceluy mort LONOLE donra topique,
Et à son fils le regne demandé.

Quatrain 10,41

En la frontiere de Caussa & de Charlus,
Non guieres loing du fonds de la valee:
De ville franche musique à son de luths,
Enuironnez combouls & grand mittee.

Quatrain 10,42

Le regne humain d'Angelique geniture,
Fera son regne paix vnion tenir:
Captiue guerre demy de sa closture,
Long temps la paix leur fera maintenir.

Quatrain 10,43

Le trop bon temps trop de bonté royale,
Fais & deffais prompt subit negligence.
Legier croira faux d'espouse loyalle,
Luy mis à mort par beneuolence.

Quatrain 10,44

Par lors qu'vn Roy sera contre les siens,
Natifs de Bloys subiuguera Ligures,
Mammel, Cordube & les Dalmatiens,
Des sept puis l'ôubre à Roy estrênes & lemeures.

Quatrain 10,46

Vie soit mort de l'or vilaine indigne,
Sera de Saxe non nouueau electeur:
De Brunsuic mandra d'amour signe,
Faux le rendant au peuple seducteur.

Quatrain 10,48

Du plus profond de l'Espaigne enseigne,
Sortant du bout & des fins de l'Europe,
Troubles passant aupres du pont de Laigne,
Sera deffaicte par bande sa grand troupe.

Quatrain 10,49

Iardin du monde aupres de cité neufue,
Dans le chemin des montaignes cauees:
Sera saisi & plongé dans la Cuve,
Beuuant par force eaux soulphre enuenimees.

Quatrain 10,53

Les trois pelices de loing s'entrebatront,
La plus grand moindre demeurera à l'escoute:
Le grand Selin n'en sera plus patron,
Le nommera feu pelte blanche routte.

Quatrain 10,54

Nee en ce monde par concupine fertiue,
A deux haut mise par les tristes nouuelles,
Entre ennemis sera prinse captiue,
Et amenee à Malings & Bruxelles.

Quatrain 10,55

Les malheureuses nopces celebreront
En grande ioye mais la fin malheureuse,
Mary & mere nore desdaigneront,
Le Phybe mort, & nore plus piteuse.

Quatrain 10,56

Prelat royal son baissant trop tiré,
Grand fleux de sang sortira par sa bouche,
Le regne Angelicque par regne respiré,
Long temps mort vifs en Tunis cômme souche.

Quatrain 10,58

Au temps du dueil que le felin monarque
Guerroyera la ieune Aemathien:
Gaule bransler, perecliter la barque,
Tenter Phossens au Ponant entretien.

Quatrain 10,59

Dedans Lyon vingtcinq d'vne haleine,
Cinq citoyens Germains, Bressans, Latins:
Par dessous noble conduiront longue traine.
Et descouuers par abbois de mastins.

Quatrain 10,60

Ie pleure Nisse, Mannego, Pize, Gennes,
Sauonne, Sienne, Capuë Modene, Malte:
Le dessus sang, & glaiue par estrennes,
Feu, trembler terre, eau. malheureuse nolte.

Quatrain 10,62

Pres de Sorbin pour assaillir Ongrie,
L'heraut de Brudes les viendra aduertir:
Chef Bisantin, Sallon de Sclauonie,
A loy d'Arabes les viendra conuertir.

Quatrain 10,63

Cydron, Raguse, la cité au sainct Hieron,
Reuerdira le medicant secours:
Mort fils de Roy par mort de deux heron,
L'Arabe, Hongrie feront vn mesme cours.

Quatrain 10,65

O vaste Rome ta ruyne s'approche,
Non de tes murs, de ton sang & substance
L'aspre par lettres fera si horrible coche,
Fer pointu mis à tous iusques au manche.

Quatrain 10,66

Le chef de Londres par regne l'Americh,
L'Isle d'Escosse tempiera par gelee:
Roy Reb auront vn si faux Antechrist,
Que les mettra trestous dans la meslee.

Quatrain 10,67

Le tremblement si fort au mois de may,
Saturne, Caper, Iupiter, Mercure au boeuf:
Venus aussi, Cancer, Mars, en Nonnay,
Tombera gresle lors plus grosse qu'vn oeuf.

Quatrain 10,70

L'oeil par obiect fera telle excroissance,
Tant & ardante que tombera la neige:
Champ arrousé viendra en decroissance,
Que le primat succombera à Rege.

Quatrain 10,71

La terre & lair geleront si grand eau,
Lors qu'on viendra pour Ieudy venerer:
Ce qui sera iamais ne fut si beau,
Des quatre parts le viendront honorer.

Quatrain 10,72

L'an mil neuf cens nonante neuf sept mois,
Du ciel viendra vn grand Roy d'effrayeur:
Resusciter le grand Roy d'Angolmois,
Auant apres Mars regner par bon-heur.

Quatrain 10,73

Le temps present auecques le passé,
Sera iugé par grand Iouialiste:
Le monde tard luy sera lassé,
Et desloyal par le clergé iuriste.

Quatrain 10,74

Au reuolu du grand nombre septiesme,
Apparoistra au temps ieux d'Hecatombe:
Non esloigné du grand aage milliesme,
Que les entrez sortiront de leur tombe.

Quatrain 10,75

Tant attendu ne reuiendra iamais,
Dedans l'Europe en Asie apparoistra:
Vn de la ligue yssu du grand Hermes,
Et sur tous Roys des Orients croistra.

Quatrain 10,78

Subite ioye en subite tristesse,
Sera à Rome aux graces embrassees:
Dueil, cris, pleurs, larm. sang, excellent liesse
Contraires bandes surprinses & troussees.

Quatrain 10,79

Les vieux chemins seront tous embellys,
Lon passera à Memphis somentree:
Le grand Mercure d'Hercules fleur de lys,
Faisant trembler terre, mer & contree.

Quatrain 10,81

Mis tresors temple citadins Hesperiques,
Dans iceluy retiré en secret lieu:
Le temple ouurir les liens fameliques,
Reprens, rauis, proye horrible au milieu.

Quatrain 10,82

Cris, pleurs, larmes viendront auec couteaux,
Semblant fuyr, donront dernier assaut,
L'entour parques planter profonds plateaux,
Vifs repoussez & meurdris de plinsaut.

Quatrain 10,83

De batailler ne sera donné signe,
Du parc seront contraints de sortir hors:
De Gand l'entour sera cogneu l'ensigne,
Qui fera mettre de tous les siens à morts.

Quatrain 10,85

Le vieil tribun au point de la trehemide
Sera pressee, captif ne deliurer,
Le vueil, non vueil, le mal parlant timide,
Par legitime à ses amis liurer.

Quatrain 10,86

Comme vn gryphon viendra le Roy d'Europe,
Accompagné de ceux d'Aquilon,
De rouges & blancs conduira grand troupe,
Et iront contre le Roy de Babylon.

Quatrain 10,87

Grând Roy viendra prendre port pres de Nisse,
Le grand empire de la mort si en fera
Aux Antipolles, posera son genisse,
Par mer la Pille tout esuanouyra.

Quatrain 10,89

De brique en mabre seront les murs reduits,
Sept & cinquante annees pacifiques:
Ioye aux humains, renoué l'aqueduict,
Santé, temps grands fruicts, ioye & mellifiques.

Quatrain 10,90

Cent fois mourra le tyran inhumain,
Mis à son lieu sçauant & debonnaire,
Tout le Senat sera dessous sa main,
Fasché sera par malin temeraire.

Quatrain 10,91

Clergé Romain l'an mil six cens & neuf,
Au chef de l'an feras election:
D'vn gris & noir de la Compagnie yssu,
Qui onc ne fut si maling.

Quatrain 10,92

Deuant le pere l'enfant sera tué,
Le pere apres entre cordes de ionç
Geneuois peuple sera esuertue,
Gisant le chef au milieu comme vn tronc.

Quatrain 10,93

La barque neufue receura les voyages,
Là & aupres transfereront l'Empire:
Beaucaire, Arles retiendrons les hostages,
Pres deux colomnes trouuees de Porphire.

Quatrain 10,94

De Nismes d'Arles, & Vienne contemner,
N'obeyr à ledict d'Hespericque:
Aux labouriez pour le grand condamner,
Six eschappez en habit seraphicque.

Quatrain 10,95

Dans les Espaignes viendra Roy trespuissant,
Par mer & terre subiugant or Midy:
Ce ma fera, rabaissant le croissant,
Baisser les aisles à ceux du Vendredy.

Quatrain 10,96

Religion du nom de mers vanicra,
Contre la secte fils Adaluncatif,
Secte obstinee deploree craindra
Des deux blessez par Aleph & Aleph.

Quatrain 10,97

Triremes pleines tout aage captif,
Temps bon à mal, le doux pour amertume:
Proye à Barbares trop tost seront hatifs,
Cupid de voir plaindre au vent la plume.

Quatrain 10,98

La splendeur claire à pucelle ioyeuse,
Ne luyra plus, long temps sera sans sel:
Auec marchans, ruffiens, loups odieuse,
Tous pesle mesle monstre vniuersel.

Quatrain 10,99

La fin le loup, le lyon, beuf, & l'asne,
Timide dama seront auec mastins:
Plus ne cherra à eux la douce manne,
Plus vigilance & custode aux mastins.

Quatrain 10,100

Le grand empire sera par Angleterre,
Le pempotam des ans de trois cens:
Grandes copies passer par mer & terre,
Les Lusitains n'en seront par contens.

Version History

Originally Completed- 2/17/1999

Revised- 7/11/2004, 12/31/2010, 5/13/2012

First Print Edition- 6/15/2012

First Digital Edition- 7/23/2013

Second Edition Completed with French text- 10/31/2022

Second Print Edition- 11/19/2022

Second Digital Edition– 11/14/2022

LES VRAYES CENTVRIES

ET PROPHETIES

De Maiftre MICHEL NOSTRADAMVS.

CENTVRIE PREMIERE.

1.

ESTANT aſſis, de nuict ſecret eſtude,
Seul; repoſe ſur la ſelle d'airain ?
Flambe exigue, ſortant de ſolitude
Fait proferer qui n'eſt à croire en vain.

2.
La verge en main miſe au milieu des branches,
De l'onde il mouille & le limbe & le pied,
Vn peur & voix fremiſſent par les manches,
Splendeur divine, le devin pres s'aſſied.

3.
Quand la lictiere du tourbillon verſée
Et feront faces de leurs manteaux couverts:
La republique par gens nouveaux vexée,
Lors blancs & rouges jugeront à l'envers.

4.
Par l'univers ſera fait un Monarque,
qu'en paix & vie ne ſera longuement,
Lors ſe perdra la piſcature barque,
Sera regie en plus grand detriment.

5.
Chaſſez ſeront ſans faire long combat,
Par le pays ſeront plus fort grevez:
Bourg & Cité auront plus grand debat
Carcas, Narbonne, auront cœurs eſprouvez.

A

A facsimile of the First Century of The Oracles of Nostradamus, Les Vrais Centuries et Propheties de Maitre Michel Nostradamus, printed in Paris 1669

About the Author

Doktor Jacqueline Dilworth has been involved in creative endeavors throughout her life and is an educator, producer, writer, filmmaker, and performer.

Her day job is as a teacher of English, Drama, and Communications to children, young adults, and adults. At night, she produces The Jackalope Hour, a radio show with music and words from across the universe and Darque Party, a radio show that features darkwave, gothic rock, and alternative rock music.

She also produces and creates videos of all kinds. Jackie writes novels, poetry, plays, as well as translates works from French into English (like the Oracles of Nostradamus or Charles Baudelaire's Bad Flowers). The Doktor has also produced and coordinated art shows such as the first versions of NADAdada, The Medusa Show, The Iris Room, and The Room of Silence.

You can visit her websites at www.mortacious.org or www.darqueparty.com

Jackie Dilworth, making a coffee forecast under the famous Reno Arch. June 2021.

www.ingramcontent.com/pod-product-compliance
Lightning Source LLC
Chambersburg PA
CBHW051751040426
42446CB00007B/307